Entrepreneurial
LEAP

Entrepreneurial

LEAP

Do You Have What It Takes to Become an Entrepreneur?

GINO WICKMAN

BenBella Books, Inc.
Dallas, TX

MyVision Clarifier™, MyBiz Match™, The Entrepreneur-in-the-Making Assessment™, The Leap Journal™, and The Six Essential Traits of an Entrepreneur™ are all trademarks of Gino Wickman.

EOS®, The Entrepreneurial Operating System®, and EOS Implementer® are all registered trademarks of EOS Worldwide, LLC.

BenBella Books, Inc.
10440 N. Central Expressway, Suite 800
Dallas, TX 75231
www.benbellabooks.com
Send feedback to feedback@benbellabooks.com

Printed in the United States of America
10 9 8 7 6 5 4 3 2

Library of Congress Cataloging-in-Publication Data:
Names: Wickman, Gino, author.
Title: Entrepreneurial Leap: do you have what it takes to become an entrepreneur? / Gino Wickman.
Description: Dallas, TX : BenBella Books, Inc., [2019] | Includes bibliographical references and index.
Identifiers: LCCN 2019019260 (print) | LCCN 2019022326 (ebook) | ISBN 9781948836814 (trade cloth : alk. paper) | ISBN 9781948836845 (ebook)
Subjects: LCSH: Entrepreneurship. | New business enterprises. | Success in business.
Classification: LCC HD62.5 .W4875 2019 (print) | LCC HD62.5 (ebook) | DDC 658.1/1—dc23
LC record available at https://lccn.loc.gov/2019019260
LC ebook record available at https://lccn.loc.gov/2019022326

Copyediting by Ginny Glass
Proofreading by Jenny Bridges and Amy Zarkos
Text design and composition by Katie Hollister

Graphic design by Drew Robinson Spork Design
Printed by Lake Book Manufacturing

Distributed to the trade by Two Rivers Distribution, an Ingram brand
www.tworiversdistribution.com

Special discounts for bulk sales are available.
Please contact bulkorders@benbellabooks.com.

To all who have taken the entrepreneurial leap. This book is a tribute to you.

CONTENTS

PART III. PATH

Setting the Stage

Taking the entrepreneurial leap is like jumping out of a plane. It's scary, exciting, half-crazy, exhilarating, risky, and rewarding.

Entrepreneurs create the most jobs, are a driving force in the economy, possess a large portion of the wealth, and spearhead much of the innovation that changes the world.

The fact that you're reading this book means that you, or someone you know, thinks you might be an entrepreneur-in-the-making. If you are, this book will show you the incredible possibilities that are available, so you can live the life you were born to live.

Three decades ago, I was right where you are. As an entrepreneur-in-the-making, I was different from others. I felt lost, confused, insecure, and out of place. After I graduated high school, my friends went off to college to get their degrees; I wanted to get to work and go make money. Looking back, I would have appreciated having a book like this one—first to help me identify that I was an entrepreneur-in-the-making and, second, to show me the path to becoming one.

In the words of National Speakers Association Hall of Fame speaker Danielle Kennedy, "We teach what we needed the most." That is why this book was written, to teach you what I needed the most back before I took my leap.

I come from the future—your future. I work with entrepreneurs who are years ahead of where you are now. You can learn a lot from their experiences as you set off on your journey.

This book is devoted to helping you understand your true skill set, your genetic code. It will give you a clear path to fully realize your entrepreneurial potential, regardless of your age. You'll read stories of people taking their leap at fifteen, twenty-five, thirty-five, and fifty-five. You're never too old to realize your full potential.

HOW TO USE THIS BOOK

Entrepreneurial Leap is divided into three parts.

Part I: Confirm will help you decide whether you're an entrepreneur-in-the-making or not. It will paint a vivid picture of the entrepreneur's unique DNA and describe the six traits essential to being an entrepreneur. You'll then take a self-assessment to confirm whether you have these traits and what it takes to become a successful entrepreneur.

Part II: Glimpse will show you what a real entrepreneur's life looks like, as well as the unlimited potential to build whatever you want. It's meant to inspire you by showing how your life can look if you take the entrepreneurial leap. You'll see all your options—the types and sizes of businesses and industries available to you—so you can determine which ones you're drawn to. You'll read real-life stories about people like you who went from where you are now to becoming successful entrepreneurs.

Part III: Path will map the stages of the entrepreneurial journey, helping you to avoid mistakes that so many entrepreneurs make along the way. It will help you to expedite finding your passion, niche, product, service, industry, and type of business, while giving you the clarity of vision and confidence to take your leap. That will increase your odds of becoming a successful entrepreneur and help you do it in less time.

How do you know if you're an entrepreneur? You may have been creating opportunities and offering solutions for a long time without even knowing it. From age seven to eighteen, I sold candy and fireworks, shoveled snow, cut lawns, washed cars, had a paper route, and sold stained glass made by my brother. Not until I was thirty years old did I fully realize I'd been an entrepreneur all along. I wish I'd known twelve years earlier. My confidence level would have been much higher, and I'd have made faster progress. The purpose of this book is to help you figure out if you're one as soon as possible.

I've spent the past thirty years learning about entrepreneurship and then applying those lessons in growing my own businesses. I was lucky enough to have two very successful entrepreneurs as mentors: my incredible father, Floyd Wickman, who founded and built the number one real estate sales training organization in the industry; and a wonderful man named Sam Cupp, who built his companies to over $300 million in revenue. These two mentors taught me most of what I know about running a business.

I've now taught and helped thousands of others. I've written six books on helping entrepreneurs and their leaders run their businesses that have sold over one million copies. I created the Entrepreneurial Operating System (EOS), which has enabled more than a hundred thousand business owners and their leaders run better businesses and organize their people and processes.

I've successfully run and sold two businesses. One was the family business my dad founded and built. I took it over at age twenty-five, turned it around, and ran it for seven years. Then we successfully sold it. The other business, EOS Worldwide, I cofounded with my partner, Don Tinney, and after eighteen years of building it, we decided to sell.

I share this information so you'll understand that I've walked every step of the entrepreneur's path. I'm going to show you that path. All of my experience and the experiences of all of my clients and mentors have been compressed into these 200 pages to help you realize your potential.

This isn't a book on theory. It's a book from the real world. It's a thinking tool—a mental, physical, emotional, and psychological journey of exploration custom-designed for you. All the opinions, expertise, and learning come from my experiences, my clients, and my mentors. All from the actual world. The entrepreneurial world.

This book will give you a huge jump start on becoming a full-fledged entrepreneur. But first you have to decide if you're even an entrepreneur-in-the-making. Not everybody is. In fact, only a small percentage of the population has all the innate traits necessary to become a true entrepreneur.

If you confirm that you truly are, this book will give you a glimpse of what your life will look like on the path to getting there. Every career has its own path. Plumbers in the making go through apprenticeship on the path to becoming master plumbers. For doctors, the path begins with pre-med, and for attorneys, the path begins with pre-law. So let's call this path *pre-entrepreneurship*.

My intent is to help you realize total freedom and unleash your creativity so you can be 100 percent who you are and act upon your genetic code, your true skill set, and your reason for being. I want to assist you in making a huge impact on the world. As you make that impact, my hope is that you'll remain humble, grounded, real, and authentic.

WHAT IS AN ENTREPRENEUR?

The word *entrepreneur* was first used in its modern meaning by French economist Jean-Baptiste Say around 1880. He wrote, "The entrepreneur shifts economic resources out of an area of lower and into an area of higher productivity and greater yield."

In his *Entrepreneur* magazine article "The True Meaning of 'Entrepreneur,'" Steve Tobak, author of *Real Leaders Don't Follow*, says, "My go-to on-line dictionary describes an entrepreneur as 'a person who starts a *business* and is willing to *risk* loss in order to make money' or 'one who organizes, manages, and assumes the *risks* of a *business* or enterprise.' Note the common keywords *business* and *risk*. If there's no real business or risk, you're not an entrepreneur."

This book defines *entrepreneur* as someone who sees a need or an opportunity and takes the risk to start a business to fulfill or remedy that need or opportunity by creating something or improving upon an existing product or service.

As an entrepreneur, you create things that didn't exist, or you make a sizable change to something that already exists. This definition of entrepreneur also includes a second- or third-generation son or daughter who takes over a family business and takes it to the next level, perhaps doubling it in size or making a transformation in its operation.

Let's also clarify what an entrepreneur is by explaining what an entrepreneur is not.

Someone who buys one franchise location, has a lifestyle business meant primarily to maintain a base-level income, works as a freelancer or an independent contractor, is a sole proprietor, or has a side hustle is not an entrepreneur. Not by this definition. In addition, a second- or third-generation business owner who simply maintains what their forebears built also isn't an entrepreneur. Such people are self-employed and bear tremendous responsibilities, but they're not true entrepreneurs.

To qualify, they have to rapidly grow their companies from scratch or take over a family business and make truly significant changes. They're like the hundreds of entrepreneurs I've worked closely with and the tens of thousands of entrepreneurs that our organization, EOS Worldwide, has helped.

WHAT IS AN ENTREPRENEUR-IN-THE-MAKING?

Now let's define a person who has the potential to become an entrepreneur.

This is an individual with a unique set of traits possessed by all true entrepreneurs but who has not yet taken an entrepreneurial leap. If you're one of them, this book will show you a path to take that first step and fulfill what you're meant to become—an entrepreneur.

Many entrepreneurs-in-the-making are young—but not all. You might be a stay-at-home mom or dad, someone who has grown restless in the corporate world, in the military, perhaps unemployed, or even homeless. You might be middle-aged and just never acted on the potential you feel inside. I'm happy to tell you that entrepreneurship is an equal-opportunity way of life. You can become an entrepreneur at any age and from any circumstance: rich or poor, employed or not.

If you're a parent or guardian and are wondering if your son, daughter, niece, or nephew is an entrepreneur-in-the-making, this book will help you find out. If you're an educator of future entrepreneurs, this book can serve as an insightful resource for you and your students.

THE NATURE OF ENTREPRENEURSHIP

The beauty of entrepreneurship is that there's no entitlement, tenure, or seniority—no pension or guarantees. It's the great equalizer, perfect and pure. Doing well doesn't depend on your past, present, or future. It only depends on the value you're bringing to the world right now. If you bring no value, you get nothing. If you bring incredible value, you reap the rewards.

Entrepreneurship doesn't care about your feelings. There are no handouts or freebies. That's why only a small percentage of the population is cut out for it.

If you have the six essential entrepreneurial traits, this book was written for you. To give you a sneak peek, here they are:

1. Visionary
2. Passionate
3. Problem solver
4. Driven
5. Risk taker
6. Responsible (blame no one)

We'll do a deep dive into each of these six essential traits to lay out what you need to know about yourself at your core.

Unfortunately, these six traits can't be taught. You're either born with them, or you're not. This book isn't going to teach you how to develop these traits, because they can't be developed. If you do possess these essential traits, this book will, first, help you confirm that you're an entrepreneur-in-the-making, and then show you how to harness and maximize your inborn abilities.

I should point out that while these traits can't be taught, they can be discovered. Someone may have given you this book because they see something in you that you don't quite see in yourself—at least not yet.

If you have these six traits, but you're not ready to take the leap, that's okay. At least you'll know that you're an entrepreneur-in-the-making and can move forward when you're ready. I didn't fully take my leap until age twenty-five. Some don't take their leap until they're in their fifties. And that's perfectly fine. Sometimes just knowing you have what it takes starts the process of turning dreams into reality.

LOOKING AHEAD

Dreams don't go very far, though. Being an entrepreneur is hard. Really hard. If you don't have the ability to roll with the inevitable punches, you'll get knocked out. Don't become an entrepreneur because it's cool. That won't work. The failure rate is high. Only about half of start-ups make it through the first five years. That's the same odds as a coin toss. Become an entrepreneur because it's your calling.

While entrepreneurship is hard, the process of becoming one is simple—but please understand that simple doesn't mean easy. Entrepreneurship means much more than new apps, technology, famous names, and billionaires. People with the essential set of entrepreneurial traits have existed on this planet for thousands of years and, by all measures, will continue to exist for thousands more. Entrepreneurs capitalize on trends, creating industries that are always changing. In the 1800s, they seized upon opportunities in railroad, telegraph, and manufacturing industries during the Industrial Revolution. In the early 1900s, they revolutionized the use of automobiles, gas, and oil. In the 1920s, they engaged in bootlegging. In the 1980s, they leveraged the computer revolution. Today, they develop apps and high tech.

Who knows what entrepreneurs will be creating in the next thirty years? The only surefire constant is that if you're an entrepreneur, you'll be capitalizing on whatever opportunity the world puts in front of you. You might be helping people live to 150, populating other planets, devising artificial intelligence, creating robots that run the world, connecting our brains to the internet, or engaging in time travel or human teleportation. Whatever you decide, the constant is that you'll be solving problems and filling needs. And getting people to pay for the solutions.

Your solutions don't have to be revolutionary or the "next big thing." You might make an impact by applying new technologies to mature industries like construction, restaurants, or distribution.

I want your abilities to serve you for a lifetime, not just for the current or next fad. Taking control of your fate does not depend on the product, service, or industry. Those all change. It relies on you knowing what you are and how to capitalize on that.

So let's find out if you're an entrepreneur-in-the-making. If you are, you'll then see what your life can look like, and then I'll show you a path for taking your leap and building your business.

Let's begin your journey . . .

PART I
CONFIRM

The purpose of part I is first to make sure that you are in fact an entrepreneur-in-the-making. We'll explore exactly what an entrepreneur is and then define the six essential traits of all entrepreneurs.

I'll paint a vivid picture of what an entrepreneur is so that you can touch it, feel it, see it, and taste it. You can then see if it resonates with you. If the picture describes qualities you have, you can then use an assessment tool to confirm if you're an entrepreneur-in-the-making.

To be frank, I'm going to do everything in my power to scare you away from becoming an entrepreneur. That's because going out on your own is hard. If you don't have all of the essential traits, you can choose from hundreds of other career options, and you'll excel at one of them. If you aren't cut out to be an entrepreneur but still decide to take the entrepreneurial leap because you want it so badly, the outcome will be excruciating. You may think it would be cool to be an entrepreneur and make a lot of money, but your odds of failure will be very high, and you'll be miserable. In the '70s and '80s, everyone wanted to be a rock star; nowadays everyone wants to be an entrepreneur.

Imagine someone who wants to be a professional singer—the next big thing—but can't carry a tune. Watch any of the televised singing competition tryouts. It's heartbreaking to hear a failed contestant say, "But this is my dream."

True entrepreneurs don't chase becoming an "entrepreneur." They instead chase their ideas and dreams, and work hard to make them a reality. And as a by-product, they're considered entrepreneurs.

So understand that if you don't have the fundamental traits required, it's okay not to become an entrepreneur. I'll never become a doctor, lawyer, police officer, paramedic, politician, or accountant, because I don't have those essential traits. It's critical for you to be honest about your abilities. It would be easy to lie to yourself while taking the assessment. Don't. I can't fill it out for you, nor can anyone else.

One way or another, the truth will set you free.

Remember: the definition of an entrepreneur is someone who sees a need or an opportunity, and then takes a risk to start a business to fulfill it.

These people are what I call "true" entrepreneurs. It's important to make a distinction between being self-employed and being a "true" entrepreneur. The best way to describe the difference is to think of a range. On the right end of the range are some of the greatest entrepreneurs of all time: Steve Jobs, Thomas Edison, and Walt Disney, to name a few. And on the left end are self-employed sole proprietors who own one franchise location, work as freelancers, are independent contractors, have a side hustle that makes a few bucks, or who have lifestyle businesses (which are businesses intended to maintain a base-level income and rarely grow). Being anywhere on this spectrum is admirable and respectable. These people are all taking a personal risk.

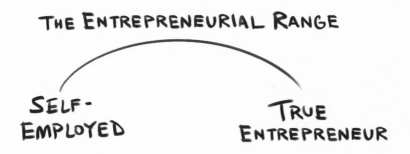

THE ENTREPRENEURIAL RANGE

SELF-
EMPLOYED

TRUE
ENTREPRENEUR

The six essential traits define entrepreneurs on the right half of the range. I'm not saying you must be the next John D. Rockefeller, just more to the right than the left. That's who this book is written for.

If at the end of part I you've confirmed that you're indeed an entrepreneur-in-the-making, I'll be happy to welcome you to the tribe. Entrepreneurs are unique. It's almost as if we're from a different planet. When you're around fellow entrepreneurs, you tend to click, speak the same language, and feel comfortable with each other.

There are many organizations that support and train entrepreneurs, such as the Entrepreneurs' Organization (EO), Young Presidents' Organization (YPO), Women Presidents' Organization (WPO), The Alternative Board (TAB), National Association of Women Business Owners (NAWBO), Vistage, the Strategic Coach® Program, and the Young Entrepreneur Council (YEC).

I was a member of the Entrepreneurs' Organization (EO) for eight years, and I remain a twenty-plus-year student of Dan Sullivan's Strategic Coach® Program. Whether I'm attending a Strategic Coach® workshop, a monthly forum meeting at EO, or meeting with my entrepreneur friends, I feel like I've arrived on my planet. We act alike, talk alike, and think alike. It's refreshing. Most other people just don't get me, and I feel a little alien and different around them. That's why it's nice to be able to go back to my planet on a regular basis.

It's the same way that other people feel when they gather with like-minded peers who have the same wiring, for instance, sports fans, robotics enthusiasts, Comic-Con fanatics, gamers, musicians, artists, fashion lovers, and foodies. They click when they're interacting together.

Let's now move forward and find out if you're an entrepreneur-in-the-making.

CHAPTER 1

KNOW THYSELF

"**W**here the needs of the world and your talents cross, there lies your vocation."

It's now time to see if your natural characteristics and "talents" are those of an entrepreneur. This chapter will give you a big picture context. The objective is to see if the descriptions of an entrepreneur resonate with you.

You're going to apply the 80 percent rule. If 80 percent of what's described in this chapter defines you, there's a good chance you're an entrepreneur at heart.

That's only the first step, though. In the following chapter, we'll define an entrepreneur's six essential traits. At that point, the 100 percent rule will take over. It's all or nothing from then on. You either have those six traits, or you don't. Let's begin now and see if entrepreneurship is your calling.

As the words inscribed above the entrance to the Temple of Apollo at Delphi in ancient Greece put it: "Know thyself."

THE CHARACTERISTICS OF AN ENTREPRENEUR

An entrepreneur is an idea generator, a dreamer. You have lots of ideas, both good and bad. No one gets it right all of the time. You're very creative and great at coming up with solutions and improvements, either by creating something new or improving on something that already exists. You're a learner. You're curious. You enjoy discovering new things and learning about them. You want to grow, reach, push the envelope. You're more comfortable with the discomfort of stretching than the contentment of the status quo.

You see the big picture. You're able to connect the dots, an ability that's almost a sixth sense. You have street smarts and common sense. Your mind-set is one that's always thinking about the future. You make decisions from your gut, and they're usually proven right, or you push hard to make them right.

You're a great strategic thinker and very persuasive. When you lock in on an objective, nothing stops you. You win people over with your passion and excitement for the project at hand. You're inspirational to those around you, whether selling them something or getting them to follow you and your thinking.

You're also passionate and obsessive. When you get focused

on an idea, a problem to solve, a product to create, or something to build, you have unlimited energy. Once you see an image in your mind, there's no stopping you, regardless of whether what you see is actually possible or not. You're an optimist, and believe every cloud has a silver lining. This is a common entrepreneurial trait.

An entrepreneur has a strong work ethic. You can out-work almost anyone. You lose track of time when you're focused on accomplishing a goal. You're driven, ambitious, and self-motivated. A fire burns inside you, and you have a tremendous sense of urgency. A hunger. A desire to be successful. You're relentless.

You're financially motivated and want to make a lot of money. Not because you're greedy, but because you want to provide for your family, yourself, and others. You have a burning desire to be financially independent. It's unfortunate that wanting to make a lot of money sometimes has a negative connotation. In the early 1900s, many people wanted to be millionaires, and becoming one was respected. My experience is that most entrepreneurs want to make a lot of money, and most are extremely generous with their money. As marketing guru Joe Polish says, "Entrepreneurs solve problems for a profit."

You have the toughness to stick it out. Angela Duckworth, in her book *Grit*, defines *grit* as "passion and perseverance in pursuit of long-term goals." She makes the point that "success rarely comes about because of intelligence, IQ, or even talent. Grit is the determining factor of success. I've never met a true entrepreneur that didn't have grit. With it comes tenacity, commitment, a strong will, dedication, stubbornness, obstinacy, determination, resiliency, and persistence."

You tend to be dominant and can be overpowering.

With your strong ambition, you're naturally competitive. Winning is important to you. You're hungry and want to be the best, so you're goal oriented and have a clear sense of urgency.

You have a strong business acumen. You may not necessarily understand a financial statement, but you see the big financial picture. Simply put, you know how to make money and have typically demonstrated this ability since a young age.

Let's look at an example of this characteristic. When Joe Haney, the founder of Sterling Insurance Group, was thirteen years old, the concrete wall that separated his family's house from their neighbors' fell into their yard. It caused quite a big mess. Joe's dad offered him $2,500 to clean up the huge pile of broken concrete, and Joe agreed to do it. Being an entrepreneur-in-the-making, Joe realized he could hire his friends to do the job and still make a nice profit.

When Joe's dad came home from work the next day, he saw Joe's friends removing the collapsed wall and asked Joe, "Why aren't you doing the work?" Joe replied, "I am." Joe's dad laughed with frustration and pride, as he knew he had an entrepreneur-in-the-making on his hands.

If you're an entrepreneur, your mind works like Joe's. You

see opportunities to make money. Not only that, but you also tended to sell stuff in your younger years, be it lemonade, candy, T-shirts, or whatever.

An entrepreneur is a risk taker, which means that once you see the opportunity, you'll take the leap, knowing there are no guarantees. You aren't afraid to challenge the status quo and be a change maker and disrupter.

You're a rebel by nature and take great pride in that. You aren't a rule follower. A stop sign to you is merely a suggestion. At the same time, you take total responsibility. While you aren't afraid to take the ball and run with it, you're totally accountable for the outcome. You blame no one else if there's a fumble.

A Geneva Business School article, "5 Tell Tale Signs You're an Entrepreneur in the Making," lists the following characteristics:

1. You don't need to be told what to do.
2. You have hobbies.
3. You act now and beg for forgiveness later.
4. You like to think outside the box.
5. You have fire.

THE CHALLENGING CHARACTERISTICS OF AN ENTREPRENEUR

By now, after reading about all these impressive characteristics, you're probably thumping your chest and standing in the Superman or Superwoman pose. But don't get too cocky. There are also some not-so-positive characteristics of entrepreneurs.

You have trouble staying focused and get bored easily. This tends to make you inconsistent. You also tend to be disorganized, a control freak, and a perfectionist. You often have ADD or ADHD, which I'm now convinced is actually a gift. You can be dyslexic; I know many entrepreneurs with dyslexia.

In his book *The Hypomanic Edge: The Link Between (a Little) Craziness and (a Lot of) Success in America*, John D. Gartner imparts an interesting theory about entrepreneurs. He says, "Part of their M.O. could be considered a form of mania." Gartner, a psychologist, in his powerful and enlightening book, shows that many of the great entrepreneurs in the past may have been hypomanic. Gartner describes hypomania as a mild form of mania that endows a person with unusual energy, creativity, enthusiasm, and a propensity for taking risks. One notable hypomanic case he cites is Andrew Carnegie, who built the American steel industry.

Gartner explains that the reason there are so many entrepreneurs in America is that most of us are immigrants. It lies in our genes because of our forebears, who had the will, optimism, and daring to leave their countries for the "promised land."

In addition to the above, entrepreneurs tend to be selfish and very independent. They can have big egos and exhibit narcissistic behaviors.

While your sixth sense makes you a revenue-generating money machine, you aren't necessarily financially savvy. You tend to spend money just as fast as you make it, and you can't make sense of a financial statement. I know many successful entrepreneurs who are flat broke after making millions because of this challenge. I was one of them at age thirty-three (more on that in the last chapter).

You may have also been labeled unfocused, learning disabled, a delinquent, or a derelict.

Dan Primack, in his *Fortune* magazine article "Antisocial Teens More Likely to Become Entrepreneurs," cites a Swedish study of grade-school kids and their paths to their midforties. It showed that, compared to other kids, male entrepreneurs often go through a stronger rebellious and nonconformist phase in adolescence.

Dr. Edward Hallowell, psychiatrist and former faculty member at Harvard Business School, says in a *Success* magazine article that the entrepreneurial brain has "pop." In his formula, pop = grit + imagination + optimism. People who start their own business have "pop." They never give up. They keep inventing new solutions and believe in the pot of gold. Dr. Hallowell has spent over thirty years working with entrepreneurs around the world. He helps them capitalize on their massive psychological strengths and minimize the carnage that can be wreaked by their weaknesses. Hallowell goes onto say that most entrepreneurs hate introspection, and even more *planning*. They prefer to operate spontaneously and, as Nike put it, "Just Do It." Over time, this tendency has led to the demise of many overnight successes.

SUMMARY

So there you have it. That is an entrepreneur in a nutshell. That six-page description can be summarized with one phrase: *the entrepreneurial spirit.* If this resonates with you, you probably have that spirit.

Now that the description has been laid out, you have to decide if it portrays you or not, applying the 80 percent rule. That is, if you have 80 percent of the qualities I've shared in this chapter, you're probably an entrepreneur-in-the-making.

Assuming you fit the bill, let's now get real. If you have these characteristics, no matter what your current status is (student, employed, unemployed, stay-at-home-parent, grandparent), you think differently from most people around you and probably always have. As a result, you're probably facing some psychological issues. You might be feeling, or have always felt, different, scared, uncertain, confused, unclear, or unsure. You may have low self-esteem or feel lost at this point in your life, even if you're putting a good face on and acting confident for the people around you: your parents, family, and friends. If that's the case, all of these emotions are normal. You're normal.

I was feeling every one of them until I was in my thirties, and I put on a good show for everyone. I'm not ashamed to admit I was downright scared. Let's face it: with the above characteristics, I was basically unemployable.

You shouldn't let any psychological issues dissuade you from taking stock of yourself and learning if you're an entrepreneur-in-the-making or not. In other words, you have to separate your emotions from your entrepreneurial characteristics, so you can make the right decision for yourself. If you don't have at least 80 percent of those characteristics, please don't take an entrepreneurial leap. That road isn't right for you.

Now that you know what an entrepreneur looks like—and even better, think you may be one—let's crystallize the picture by making absolutely sure you have the six essential traits of an entrepreneur.

CHAPTER 2

THE SIX ESSENTIAL TRAITS OF AN ENTREPRENEUR

This is where the decision-making process gets real. In the previous chapter, when reading about entrepreneurial characteristics and applying the 80 percent rule, you still had some wiggle room to maybe kid yourself. In this chapter, it's all or nothing: 100 percent or no deal. You either have the six essential traits, or you don't.

A *trait* is defined as a "genetically determined characteristic." That means a trait's in your DNA. It's your natural wiring. We aren't talking about skills here. Skills can be learned; traits can't.

You're either born with certain traits, or you aren't. To help you relate, traits are also known as characteristics, attributes, features, qualities, properties, and mannerisms. While we regard these terms as positive, traits are also known as idiosyncrasies, peculiarities, quirks, oddities, or foibles because these words are all synonyms of the word *trait*. They can be perceived positively or negatively, depending on who is doing the judging. Said another way, some people will consider your entrepreneurial traits odd and quirky. When they do, take it as a compliment, not a criticism.

Essential is defined as "absolutely necessary, extremely important." These are *essential* traits. You have to have them if you're going to become a true entrepreneur!

I know this book is going to break a few hearts. I take no pleasure in that, but when I help someone realize that they aren't an entrepreneur, I'm doing them a service. I'm not only saving them years of pain. I'm moving them one step closer to figuring out their true calling.

This caution in no way is intended to fire up someone to become an entrepreneur. Anyone who has each one of these six essential traits will be self-motivated. You shouldn't try to psyche yourself up to become someone you're not. That's not only counterproductive but also destructive. As an analogy, the late Jim Rohn, who was both an entrepreneur and motivational speaker, said, "Motivation alone is not enough. If you have an idiot and you motivate him, now you have a motivated idiot." While that may be a bit harsh, hopefully, it makes the point.

So let's dive into the six essential traits.

THE FIRST ESSENTIAL TRAIT: VISIONARY

This trait is sometimes hard to understand because it's so broad, or you simply may not be comfortable saying you're something as grand as a "visionary." During an interview with one entrepreneur, he said humbly, "I really don't think I'm a visionary." This is a man who built a $40 million company from scratch. He absolutely is a visionary.

This trait is measured by your ability to connect the dots, see the big picture, and envision the future. Visionary is defined as being imaginative, creative, inventive, ingenious, enterprising, and innovative. You're a dreamer. You have a sixth sense for resolving the problem you're focused on. Simply put, you have ideas.

You have the intuitive ability to know how to make money and understand how economics work at a very high level. You have common sense, business sense, and street smarts. You're able to see around corners, and you have a future-oriented mind-set.

Visionary doesn't mean you have to be Thomas Edison or that you'll invent the next iPhone. I teach entrepreneurs a tool called the "visionary spectrum," which illustrates how much of a visionary a company needs—because not every company needs an Elon Musk. If you think about the spectrum's high and low ends, the high end might be a high-tech company and the low end might be a property management company.

THE VISIONARY SPECTRUM

HIGH (HIGH-TECH)

LOW (PROPERTY MANAGEMENT)

How much visionary a business needs is determined by the (1) type of industry, (2) growth aspirations, and (3) the degree of market dynamics (change, competition, or complexity) a company will encounter. When you combine these three factors, you'll find where your business is on the visionary spectrum. If all these factors are red-lined, you might need to be an Elon Musk. If not, that level of visionary is probably not necessary.

David Allen had just the right amount of visionary to build The Allen Groupe into the premier private-jet cleaning business in the industry. He built it based on a chain of events that began when he was an entrepreneur-in-the-making at fifteen years old.

David started off by cleaning cars to make money. He quickly evolved to detailing cars. At sixteen, when he detailed his dad's car, his father was so impressed that he agreed to buy David's necessary supplies, equipment, and cleaning chemicals to go fully into auto detailing.

David was making a hefty $300–$400 per week during his teens when another opportunity presented itself. Because he lived near the Indianapolis Speedway, he received offers to clean motor homes for the drivers at the Indy race events, and that step evolved into cleaning large trucks and trailers. His work became so popular that he was invited to travel to other Indy car race events in other states to clean trucks and trailers. He continued this through college.

His big chance came when he was offered a further opportunity. One of his clients asked him to clean three jets for a private owner. He was trained on the intricacies of jet cleaning, and he applied some of his prior skills to the jet-cleaning business. He started getting referrals, and the jet-cleaning business grew.

He took the opportunity very seriously. He went above and beyond studying, learning, and getting certified in all aspects of cleaning. He built such a great reputation that he was approached by NetJets, a company that sells fractional ownership of private jets and has locations in many major cities. After he completed their audit process, they were so impressed that they immediately gave David the contract for their Orlando, Florida, location.

David then truly revolutionized the industry by creating systems and software to clean private jets better and faster than anyone else. Along the way, he raised the level of professionalism of his cleaning staff through training, uniforms, and increased morale, ultimately attaining the highest retention rate of cleaning employees in the industry.

David grew the company rapidly over the next fifteen years to thirty-seven locations with three hundred employees and $12 million in revenue.

Hopefully, you can see that "visionary" comes in all shapes and sizes. What's needed is a mind-set that keeps looking for opportunities, discarding what doesn't fit the evolving vision, and continuing to implement improvements as necessary.

Are you visionary?

THE SECOND ESSENTIAL TRAIT: PASSIONATE

The definition of *passionate* is "showing or caused by strong feelings or a strong belief." Passionate people believe in something strongly; you can't change their minds. Synonyms for passion are enthusiasm, love, mania, fascination, obsession, fanaticism, fixation, compulsion, appetite, and addiction.

Passionate entrepreneurs are energized by solving a problem in their industry, filling a void, fixing, helping, making a difference, building, or creating. Passion is an essential trait, because it gets an entrepreneur through tough times. You cannot survive failure without passion. Most people give up when faced with their first setback, because they're just not passionate enough about their idea, business, product, service, or customers.

Passionate means that you have passion for your product or service, your idea or deliverable.

When you have passion for what you're offering the world, you have superhuman strength that keeps your blood pumping and not only helps you endure tough times, but also motivates, persuades, inspires, and sells other people around you to act, move, and follow your lead. You simply cannot accomplish much without other people's help, and people love to follow a passionate leader.

When building EOS Worldwide, to say that I was passionate about creating a system that would help entrepreneurs get everything they want from their businesses would be a gross understatement.

For the first five years of creating the Entrepreneurial Operating System (EOS), I worked tirelessly. I obsessed every minute of every day honing, refining, and testing hundreds of ideas and options. I delivered over five hundred full-day sessions in those years, with entrepreneurs and their leadership teams, until I perfected the model. Until they loved it. Until I changed their lives.

I then spent three years writing my first book whenever I could find time, making sure that it was a complete how-to manual for anyone who wanted an operating system to run a better business. I constantly got feedback from my clients and the general public to make sure they loved it. And then spent the next ten years with my partner, Don Tinney, building a team of hundreds of EOS Implementers to spread the ideas to the world.

During this period, I definitely sacrificed family time, time with friends, and my health. Regardless, I was always driven by one overriding passion. To help those entrepreneurs have better quality of life, make more money, do what they love, and make an impact on the world.

Passionate means that you have such a strong belief that you'll do almost anything to prove, create, or deliver your idea, product, or service to the world.

Are you passionate?

THE THIRD ESSENTIAL TRAIT: PROBLEM SOLVER

Being a problem solver is as much about new ideas, innovation, and creating things as it is about dealing with barriers, obstacles, and setbacks. A problem solver is an optimist by nature. You see solutions to everything, whether it's a product or service you create to fill a need you saw, or a setback you experience when your product fails and you reinvent it. Your mind always sees solutions.

A problem solver is always figuring out how to make something smarter, faster, less expensive, better, or higher quality. They're innovators and testers who love trial and error. When they hit a brick wall, they figure out how to go over it, around it, or through it.

A prime example of this would be the case of Bob Verdun,

who overcame two major problems during the twenty years of building his business.

Bob started his company in 1990 after resigning from a lucrative job in tech because he didn't like the way his boss treated people. He then became a contractor in the software industry, teaching resellers for a software company. As Bob was teaching these resellers, who were all entrepreneurs, he realized that he too was an entrepreneur.

He said to himself, "Are you kidding me? If they can do this, I can do this." And he started his own business. With no business plan, with no outside money, he bootstrapped a software resale company. His company, CFI, started selling, servicing, and implementing computer-aided design (CAD) software for design companies, digitizing their old paper drawings and helping companies run the software and hardware. His company had a great record of success for five years, until the competition caught up and the business became commoditized. He could see the end was coming, so he had to reinvent the business. Major problem to solve number one.

Bob morphed CFI into a service business that focused on large-scale implementations of software outside of CAD. The shift worked, and the company grew into a $28 million company. And then, unfortunately, in 2000 when the dot-com crash hit, CFI plunged from $28 million in revenue to $4 million overnight. Major problem to solve number two.

Bob had to reinvent the company once again. First, he had

to lay off many of his employees. He focused the company on generating recurring revenues through complicated software implementations for real estate companies that had multiple assets to manage. To protect the company from another downturn, he diversified the product lines and the geographical scope. The company rapidly grew again, became highly profitable, and seamlessly sailed through the great recession of 2008.

In 2015, Bob successfully sold his company.

A problem solver is someone who leans into problems, obsesses about them, and genuinely gets a high from solving them. That takes a special type of person. Most people run from their problems, avoid them, or hope they solve themselves or go away.

You have to want to solve problems. No matter how great your original vision is, bumps will appear in the road. Your industry can change, and your customers' needs can change. If you can't fix what's holding your company back, it's game over.

Are you a problem solver?

THE FOURTH ESSENTIAL
TRAIT: DRIVEN

The definition of *driven* is "operated, moved, or controlled by a specific source of power." Driven people have a strong sense of urgency. This trait is essential to success. Whether you're trying to prove something to someone, trying to avoid the life you had growing up, or trying not to be a failure, these are some of the roots of an entrepreneur's drive.

This trait is very different from the trait of passion. Whereas being passionate is about passion for your product or service, being driven is about an internal fire that you want to succeed, regardless of what the product or service is.

At a meeting of entrepreneurs, the host brought in four of his newest employees for a Q & A session. All were very driven, hardworking people in their early twenties. We peppered these young ambitious people with questions. I asked them where they got their strong work ethic and drive. While each answer was a little different, in every case they went back to a very young age—before they were ten years old—to recount where their drive came from. The point is that you've either had this trait for as long as you can remember—and have always exhibited it—or you don't have it.

Driven people are tenacious, competitive, self-motivated, goal-oriented, growth-oriented, and never give up. They hustle. They want to succeed.

A good example of someone with drive is Zac Voss. In his final year of college at the University of Iowa while doing some marketing for bars and restaurants, he had his light bulb moment.

A friend of his came back from a trip to Spain and told him about the hottest drink going there. It was a new beverage called Red Bull.

They bought a case over the internet from Red Bull direct,

at a cost of over fifty dollars per case with shipping. When Zac's customer found out how expensive the product was, he refused to purchase more. Not willing to fail, Zac called the phone number on the website and asked how he could get it for less. He was informed, "You can't, because there are no distributors in Iowa."

So Zac said, "You're talking to him. What do you need me to do?" Zac was given a name and a phone number, which happened to be the CEO of Red Bull North America.

He called countless times, to no avail and no return calls, until he finally got the CEO to take his call. He offered Zac the opportunity to participate in a "market-seeding program" where Zac would introduce the product into his marketplace with no guarantees, no contracts, and he had to follow their rules. If that worked out, there might be a distributor opportunity in the future.

Zac took the deal and went to work. He set up his friends to sell the product in four different cities across the state. He soon was outselling every other seeding program in the country. Zac was determined to get his distributorship. He wrote a business plan. He created a mock-up of a Red Bull can with his pitch and brand promise printed on the can. He then sent the package to the CEO asking for a distributorship in Iowa.

The CEO was so impressed. Zac's persistence finally paid off. He officially owned his own distributor company. He now has a fleet of sixty vehicles and more than a hundred employees who sell to about five thousand retail outlets in Iowa, Illinois, and Missouri.

Driven means not settling for second best. You're relentless. In order for your business to be successful, you have to want to win—because there will always be competing forces. If you only take what comes, you'll find your company slipping backward. Only your drive to succeed will break down barriers to grow to the next level.

Are you driven?

THE FIFTH ESSENTIAL TRAIT: RISK TAKER

A risk taker is someone willing to take a leap and willing to fail. A risk taker is a rule breaker, change maker, disruptor. The status quo is not good enough. Entrepreneurs take risks: calculated risks. They're willing to fail, try again, and adapt. When it comes time to take a leap, they understand the risk/reward equation and prefer to take a big risk for a big reward.

Looking at your past history, have you taken risks? Are you rebellious? This is why most people don't take an entrepreneurial leap. They have all of the other essential traits—they have an idea, are passionate, and are decent problem solvers. They're driven and responsible. But they're just afraid to take that plunge into the unknown. They're afraid of losing their shirt, afraid of failure, afraid of rocking the boat, afraid of being embarrassed in the eyes of others. When confronted with the thought of jumping out of a plane, they simply freeze.

Please be honest with yourself if this describes you.

A risk taker gets a high from changing things up, defying the norms. Risk takers are a little crazy. They're willing to fall on their faces. They don't plan or want to fail, but for them, the potential upside always outweighs the downside. As a worst case, a failure for them is a learning experience and a part of the process.

As the late Dr. David Viscott put it: "If you cannot risk, you cannot grow. If you cannot grow, you cannot become your best. If you cannot become your best, you can't be happy. If you cannot be happy, what else matters?"

One example of a risk taker is Clay Upton. In his second year of college, he realized that he wouldn't be able to graduate without first completing four semesters of a foreign language.

Clay had always had a difficult time with learning languages, and it wasn't getting any easier in college. He decided that, for him, it was counterproductive to study a language when he wasn't passionate about it. He made the risky decision to stop pursuing a degree. He knew he was making a decision that would risk his future career opportunities and earning potential. And at the same time, it opened a world of opportunity as an entrepreneur.

Although he let go of the idea of graduating, Clay stayed in college all four years. Instead of following a course of study defined by the university, he registered for courses of his choosing. In his free time, he became acquainted with the start-up community, and he built and tested companies in the areas that were interesting to him. With each company, he learned valuable market lessons.

By the time he left college with no degree, he felt he was ready to take the leap. He founded Traction® Tools, a software platform helping entrepreneurs run better businesses. Without a degree, Clay's only option was to succeed. He worked for no compensation and spent two years and all his money building the company's infrastructure and original team. When he was down to his last $400, things turned around. Traction Tools found its momentum and has been profitable ever since.

Today, despite knowing only English, he has clients in thirty-six countries and employees across six time zones.

Taking big risks isn't for most people. It petrifies them. That's why so few take the entrepreneurial leap.

Are you a risk taker?

THE SIXTH ESSENTIAL TRAIT: RESPONSIBLE (BLAME NO ONE)

Entrepreneurs take total responsibility for the outcome. They don't make excuses. They don't complain. If you possess this trait, you accept the burden of becoming completely financially accountable. You don't believe in entitlement. You never look for a handout. You're self-sufficient and self-reliant. Above all, you blame no one else for things that go wrong.

Responsible is the ability to act independently and make decisions without authorization. Synonyms for responsible are accountable and answerable.

It's one thing to be very independent. It's quite another to be willing to assume total responsibility for the outcome of a decision. When responsible entrepreneurs make a bad decision, drop the ball, or don't live up to an expectation, they're the first to say, "My bad," "That one is on me," "I'm sorry." Their default is looking in the mirror for blame, not looking at others.

Dan Sullivan, the creator of The Strategic Coach® Program, has trained thousands of entrepreneurs. He happens to be one of my mentors. His definition of an entrepreneur is someone who, first, decides they will depend on their own initiative, performance, and results to guarantee their financial security; and second, decides they won't expect anyone to give them an opportunity until they've first created something that's useful and valuable.

Responsible people know everyone is looking at them and are comfortable carrying that load.

Ted Bradshaw, a serial entrepreneur with multiple business successes, shares the following story. "I got into the custom home building business. My role was securing vacant lots in desirable, mature neighborhoods, and my business partner was responsible for building $1M+ custom homes on the land I secured. My partner went bankrupt due to some poor business dealings in another venture. I had a choice: sell the land portfolio and walk away relatively unscathed or find a way to help complete the builds for the half dozen clients that had already spent millions to have their homes built. Instead of cutting the losses and running, I spent two years making sure each of those clients found a way to get their homes built."

A responsible person typically takes the high road and does the right thing, which is often the more difficult course. They take full accountability. Even when it's sometimes easier to drop the ball and run. They grab the reins when the horses pulling the stagecoach are out of control. Just like in Greek mythology, they're similar to Atlas and are able to carry the weight of the heavens on their shoulders.

A responsible person believes that their current state (whatever it is) is a culmination of their own decisions and choices, no one else's. They default to "How do I solve *my* problem?" not "Look at what *they* did to me."

Are you responsible?

SUMMARY

Let's review the six essential traits that make up an entrepreneur's genetic coding:

1. Visionary
2. Passionate
3. Problem solver

4. Driven

5. Risk taker

6. Responsible (blame no one)

Now it's time for you to be very honest with yourself. You either answered yes to all six, or you didn't. You either are an entrepreneur-in-the-making, or you aren't.

If you are, the next three chapters will act as final filters, just to be absolutely sure. Then, in part II, we'll give you a glimpse of what your life as an entrepreneur could look like.

If you aren't an entrepreneur-in-the-making, that's okay. There's no shame in that. I hope these first chapters have given you the clarity to find your calling. In your search, please consider the words of Frederick Buechner on your calling being "where your deepest gladness and the world's deep hunger meet."

Know thyself.

CHAPTER 3

WHAT IF YOU'RE MISSING AN ESSENTIAL TRAIT?

At this point, I hope you're certain that you're an entrepreneur-in-the-making. If so, you might be saying to yourself, "Let's get to work!"

I urge you to be patient. The next three chapters provide the final filters. And truth be told, I'm still trying to scare you away.

In the title of Michael Gerber's great book, *The E-Myth Revisited: Why Most Small Businesses Don't Work and What to Do About It, e-myth* is short for the "entrepreneurial myth," that every business is started by those with business skills, when in actuality they're mostly started by technicians—and that's why they fail. Gerber says not everyone should take the leap. He describes the wrong person taking an entrepreneurial leap as having an "entrepreneurial seizure."

An employee who decides to start their own company because they're great at their job, but doesn't possess the essential traits, is having an entrepreneurial seizure. Unfortunately, in most cases they fail because they don't possess all the other characteristics, over and above the job skills that they need to succeed at being an entrepreneur.

Gerber goes on to describe the three levels of people in every company: the technician, the manager, and the entrepreneur. The technician is the employee who does the specialized work. The manager is the person who manages the systems and the people. The entrepreneur is the visionary, the opportunist, the "catalyst for change."

The point is that you must know yourself and decide. Are you really a great employee (technician)? Are you a great manager? Or are you truly an entrepreneur? If you're great at your job and are thinking of taking the entrepreneurial leap to starting your own business doing that job, make sure you aren't having an entrepreneurial seizure. Make sure you're someone with all six essential traits. Just as a gas-powered car needs an engine, transmission, wheels, a steering wheel, gas, and oil to function, the entrepreneur needs to be visionary, passionate, a problem solver, driven, a risk taker, and responsible.

Imagine not having one vital component for your car. You won't go far. The same goes for lacking an essential trait.

So, what if you're missing any one of the six essential entrepreneurial traits, but still have all of the others? Let's look at why that won't work.

NOT HAVING THE VISIONARY TRAIT

Not being visionary means you'll never really be able to connect the dots and see the big picture. You'll also struggle to create something from scratch or to continuously innovate and improve upon what already exists.

If you have all the other traits and not this one, you'll probably make a great salesperson. As a salesperson you can make a lot of money with your passion, problem-solving skills, strong work ethic, ability to take risks, and sense of responsibility.

NOT HAVING THE PASSIONATE TRAIT

If you aren't passionate about the void you're going to fill in the world with your product or service, you'll never survive the many setbacks and failures that will occur, especially in the first few years. No one has ever devised a magic formula for enduring the tough times. Only passion for your customer, offering, or solution will help you push past the barriers. That passion for your product or service gives you the energy, tenacity, and optimism to ignore the fact that the odds are stacked against you. That's what enables you to pull off what most people can't.

NOT HAVING THE PROBLEM-SOLVER TRAIT

It might seem that being visionary and passionate makes you a great problem solver. Unfortunately, they don't. I've met many "idea people" who are extremely passionate but just can't solve problems. They have their "big idea," but have no ability, desire, or interest in solving the hundreds of issues that are going to arise over the next few years of building a business—or even the one problem they will need to solve tomorrow.

Like the great boxer Mike Tyson said, "Everybody has a plan until they get punched in the mouth." A problem solver takes the punch, reassesses the plan, adjusts, keeps moving forward, and typically wins the fight. Someone who doesn't possess this trait gets rattled by the first punch and then gets their ass kicked.

A problem solver has the ability to consistently create value for their customers, clients, and employees by listening to and understanding what's not working and then fixing it.

If you don't have this essential trait, but you have all the others, you might want to buy a franchise that aligns with your passions. The beauty of a franchise is that you're buying a proven system, where the franchisor has already solved most of your problems and continues to do so as new ones arise.

NOT HAVING THE DRIVEN TRAIT

The downside of lacking this essential trait should be pretty obvious. It's the most common reason entrepreneurs fail. To succeed, you have to love working hard. Entrepreneurship means rolling up your sleeves, and most people just don't want to work that hard. They aren't self-motivated enough. Being driven means you never take your foot off the gas. You know that there are a thousand other hard workers trying to beat you and you must outwork them. You must have a burning desire to succeed.

Dan Sullivan describes those who are self-motivated as "batteries-included people." I can't tell you the number of times I've sat with "batteries-*not*-included people" who want to be successful and accomplish big goals. These people start out totally energized when I sit with them for an hour or two. During the meeting, I help them document their vision, plan the big picture, assess the money they're going to make and all the people they're going to help.

However, when we start boiling down the plan of attack and all the work that they must do in the next three months, the life completely goes out of them. They look like they need a nap, and I never hear from them again.

In case I haven't mentioned it before, entrepreneurship is hard.

NOT HAVING THE RISK-TAKER TRAIT

Many people with great ideas are very passionate, incredibly hard workers, and very responsible. But they already have a great, secure job. Or they want to wait until they save up a certain amount of money, or until the kids are in school, or until they get married, or until they're taller, or until (fill in the blank). They're just too afraid to take their leap.

Here are three decision-making philosophies:

1. It's more important that you decide than what you decide.
2. Just get it 80 percent right the first time.
3. If you have 70 percent of the information and feel 70 percent confident, move forward.

If you aren't comfortable living by those types of guidelines, you're probably not a risk taker.

Looked at another way, maybe you constantly overanalyze tough decisions and end up frozen when it's time to make the call. In that case, you'll rarely make the tough but necessary decisions that will keep your company growing. You'll typically panic when competitors are kicking your ass rather than outthinking them.

A risk taker is able to make a tough call when they know people won't agree with them and the stakes are high. The point is made in a *Fortune* magazine issue on decision making: Jim Collins, the author of *Good to Great*, said that in his years and years of research, "No major decision we've studied was ever taken at a point of unanimous agreement."

If you have all of the other traits and lack this one, partnering with a true entrepreneur might be the right decision for you.

NOT HAVING THE RESPONSIBLE TRAIT

Picture someone who is visionary, passionate, driven, a problem solver, and a risk taker, but they don't take responsibility for outcomes. They blame others when things go wrong, and they feel they're entitled to future rewards because of their past accomplishments.

A lot of people are like that. They complain that their idea would have worked if not for (fill in the blank). Or if they had (fill in the blank). These people tend to fail quickly, because the blame game quickly escalates. It creates resentment in the people around the person casting blame. Morale is always low, and employees tend to leave.

Think about whether or not you have this critical trait. When you come down to it, there are really only two types of people in the world: those who take total responsibility and those who blame others.

Think about the people in your life right now. You can put

each of them in one of these two categories. They either take total responsibility, or they don't. Most important, decide which group you're in. The reason I believe the responsible trait is genetic is that when you separate people into the two categories, you'll find siblings often divided up into each group. How can so many brothers and sisters who grew up in the same household, raised the same way, by the same parents, be so different when it comes to taking responsibility? In my opinion, the reason can only be nature over nurture.

Regardless of whether it is nature or nurture, it shows up in people at a young age and continues through their lives. In his best-selling book, *The Road Less Traveled*, M. Scott Peck, MD, describes two extremes on the responsibility spectrum. He writes, "Most people who come to see a psychiatrist are suffering from what's called either a *neurosis* or a *character disorder*. Put most simply, these two conditions are disorders of responsibility, and as such, they are opposite styles of relating to the world and its problems. The neurotic assumes too much responsibility: the person with a character disorder, not enough."

Now, I'm not a psychologist, and I'm not saying all people have a disorder. All I know is that the thousands of true entrepreneurs that I've interacted with take responsibility. Whether or not the amount of responsibility they take for things is entirely healthy, well, that's for a different book. It's just who and what they are.

If you don't have this vital trait, you might find that being a one-person show, solo entrepreneur, independent contractor, or freelancer is a better path for you. You'll have no employees to blame. While you might still blame your customers, clients, and vendors when things go wrong, at least you won't have any employees walking out on you.

SUMMARY

Now let's go back to the entrepreneurial range we laid out earlier, covering the spectrum from being self-employed to a true entrepreneur.

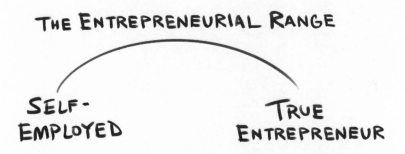

THE ENTREPRENEURIAL RANGE

SELF-EMPLOYED

TRUE ENTREPRENEUR

The six essential traits define a true entrepreneur. It's important for you to decide where you fall on that range. If you're missing a trait, you might then fall to the far left of the range.

This chapter began with a comparison of a would-be entrepreneur missing a key trait to a car missing a vital component. Not having a trait makes the success of the entrepreneurial leap highly unlikely. Just as someone who is six four and 220 pounds will probably never be a horse-racing jockey or someone who faints at the sight of blood might never become a surgeon.

If you're thinking you "sort of" fit the bill, you're probably not a true entrepreneur.

Know thyself.

Chapter 4

Second-Generation Entrepreneurs

Before turning to the Entrepreneur-in-the-Making Assessment in the next chapter (which is the final filter to confirm if you have entrepreneurial DNA), let's take a look at second- and third-generation entrepreneurs. As you recall, that's a son or daughter who takes over and transforms the family business or at least doubles it in size.

It's important to note, first off, that if you're a son or daughter who takes an entrepreneurial leap that has nothing to do with the family business, you aren't a second-generation entrepreneur: you're an entrepreneur, pure and simple. This chapter is focused only on a member of the younger generation thinking of getting involved in or taking over the family business.

It also will help an entrepreneurial parent determine if their son or daughter has the requisite entrepreneurial DNA. To be perfectly direct, if they aren't visionary, passionate, a problem solver, driven, a risk taker, and responsible, they don't.

Please feel free to skip this chapter if you have no interest in learning about multigeneration entrepreneurs.

I am adding this chapter because I've seen far too many times what happens when a nonentrepreneurial son or daughter takes over the family business. It's an excruciating experience for all involved. The next generation may feel entitled to the role, or the parent puts their kid in a leadership position because continuing the family tradition is "their dream." Being an entrepreneur is not something you can inherit. It has to be inside you no matter who your parents are.

DEFINING THE ROLE

Let's start by imagining the circumstances in which a parent would put their kid in the role of running their company. The typical reason is that the parent is ready to retire and wants to put someone in their founder/entrepreneur role.

The parent must first clearly recognize that their role will now be available to *someone*, but not necessarily their son or daughter. This will help them detach from fixating on a successor within their family.

Uncoupling that link will help the parent see more clearly what's needed. If they want the company to evolve with the times and last for decades, they'll need to fill that role with another entrepreneur—someone with the six essential traits—no matter who it is.

If the parent's objective is merely to maintain the company or let it run its course, then they can pass the company on to one of their kids even if they don't have the traits of a true entrepreneur.

However, if the company depends on your entrepreneurial abilities or your business is in an industry that's constantly evolving, your thinking has to be different. If the son or daughter doesn't have the six traits 100 percent, I urge you not to move forward. If you do, it will be painful and frustrating for all involved. Instead, fill the role with someone else who has all the requisite entrepreneurial traits. I assure you they're out there. Hopefully, it's a niece or nephew, a son- or daughter-in-law, or someone already working in your business. Worst case, you'll have to look outside the company.

If you want a nonentrepreneurial child to join the business, and they want that as well, put them in a position suitable to their skills. You must realize that it's fairly rare for a son or daughter to inherit their parent's entrepreneurial traits. Research on the subject shows that only about 32 percent of second-generation businesses survive, only about 13 percent of third-generation, and only about 3 percent of fourth-generation and beyond.

For instance, I worked with a family business in which the father wanted to transition his business to his son and daughter, neither of whom was an entrepreneur. They became my clients when the family was about two years into the transition. Already the changeover was painful for everyone. The entrepreneurial deficit created a stagnant, self-defeating dynamic. Every time the leadership team had to make a tough decision, the son would say, "Okay, let's vote." The business, like most businesses run by consensus, never grew.

On the other hand, I'm happy to say that I've seen many success stories where a daughter or son took over, and the company grew, transformed, evolved, and actually became more successful than in the previous generation.

A great example of a second-generation entrepreneur is Jay Feldman of Feldman Automotive. Jay started working in his dad's car dealership at the age of eight, washing cars and doing odds and ends. He remembers always wanting to be on the lot. On snow days at school, he didn't want to play like the other kids; he wanted to go to work at the dealership.

He started selling cars before he had a driver's license. He described himself as "extremely competitive," which he showed by becoming the top salesperson in the summer when he was sixteen years old.

After graduating college early, at age twenty, he went to work for the dealership full-time as finance manager. He quickly worked his way up to sales manager and then general manager of the dealership. In that position, he grew the dealership from $20 million in revenue to $45 million.

At age twenty-five, he and his dad became fifty-fifty partners when they moved and built a new dealership. Jay grew the newly relocated dealership to $85 million. Since then, Jay has bought his dad out and continues to buy and grow dealerships. He currently has ten dealerships, generating $1 billion in revenue and employing nine hundred people.

Now let's look at the example of a third-generation entrepreneur, Mike Uckele of Uckele Health and Nutrition. His grandfather started a supplement business focused on the health of farm production animals (cattle, swine, etc.) in 1962. In 1978, Mike's dad came into the business, and Mike's dad and uncle ran the business until 2005.

Mike first got involved in the family business in 1987 while in high school and after graduating college became involved full-time. After a decade of watching his dad and uncle bicker as partners, he offered to buy the company to solve the problem, and they took the offer.

At the time, the company was earning $4.5 million in revenue, still focusing on the health of production animals. Mike's passion about the family business cannot be overstated. He first whipped the company into shape by cutting unnecessary inventory and getting rid of bad customers. He then refocused the company to supply the equine, pet, and human supplement market. By transforming the company, he took it to another level, growing it to $50 million in revenue and 150 employees.

Another example is Gretchen Hopp Doyle of Baker-Hopp and Associates, a rare fourth-generation entrepreneur who has beaten the daunting odds. Her insurance agency was started in the early 1900s by her great-grandfather, John A. Baker, as a life insurance company that he ran out of his house.

John had four daughters involved in the business. One of his daughter's husbands (Gretchen's grandfather) had the entrepreneurial gene. He took the company over in the late 1940s.

In 1967, Gretchen's father took over the business and grew it rapidly.

At the age of twenty-five, Gretchen wanted to be an entrepreneur and business owner herself. In 1996, she joined the family business. She started in sales and worked her way up through the ranks. When her dad was ready to retire in 2006, she and a partner bought him out. Gretchen has since bought her partner out, becoming the sole owner of Baker-Hopp and Associates. She continues to successfully grow her fourth-generation business.

Kathy Kolbe and Amy Bruske's book, *Business Is Business: Reality Checks for Family-Owned Companies,* is the proverbial handbook on family businesses. Helping you decide if you should bring a family member into your business, how to bring family members into your business, managing the relationship, and removing family members from your business, Kathy and Amy state, "We've seen family-owned businesses survive economic losses, fires, tornadoes, threats, and deaths. We have never seen a family-owned business survive heirs who lack ambition."

SUMMARY

I hope this chapter will greatly improve the odds of multigenerational-family-business success. The fact that fewer than 15 percent of family-owned businesses survive through a third-generation is heartbreaking.

Finally, I'd like to offer two last pieces of advice from my personal experience as a second-generation entrepreneur. When I wanted to get involved in my family's business, a real estate sales training organization, my father was adamant that I succeed somewhere else first before coming to work for the company. He urged me to go sell $5 million in real estate, which I did. It helped greatly from several standpoints: my confidence level, the respect from his employees, and my having broader experiences.

The second piece of advice is that a second- or third-generation entrepreneur should also understand that, unfortunately, you have to work harder than anyone else in the organization to get the same level of respect. It's just the reality of being the owner's daughter or son.

Let's now move on to the Entrepreneur-in-the-Making Assessment, the final filter in determining if you have what it takes.

CHAPTER 5

THE ENTREPRENEUR-IN-THE-MAKING ASSESSMENT

Without further ado, we've come to the final piece of the puzzle. The following assessment will enable you to decide if you've got the required entrepreneurial DNA.

This assessment will only work if you answer these questions of your own free will, with no outside influences. Above all, you must be honest with yourself. If you aren't, you're only hurting yourself.

This is not like a driving test, where you get a pass/fail result. It's an assessment of whether or not you have the traits of an entrepreneur—based on your opinion, no one else's. You're ultimately the judge and jury.

THE ENTREPRENEUR-IN-THE-MAKING ASSESSMENT

Please read each statement and answer truthfully. Do you agree that the statement describes you? Please be very honest with yourself.

	Strongly Disagree	Disagree	Agree	Strongly Agree
	1	2	3	4
1. I am competitive.	☐	☐	☐	☐
2. I want to make a lot of money.	☐	☐	☐	☐
3. I work harder than other people	☐	☐	☐	☐
4. I have a lot of ideas.	☐	☐	☐	☐
5. I am self-motivated, driven, and have a strong sense of urgency.	☐	☐	☐	☐
6. I have a lot of energy.	☐	☐	☐	☐
7. I am very passionate.	☐	☐	☐	☐

8. I am very
   responsible.   ☐   ☐   ☐   ☐

9. I make tough
   decisions faster   ☐   ☐   ☐   ☐
   than most

10. I am good at per-
    suading people to   ☐   ☐   ☐   ☐
    do things.

11. I enjoy setting
    goals and am goal   ☐   ☐   ☐   ☐
    oriented.

12. I love to grow and
    learn.   ☐   ☐   ☐   ☐

13. I am a good
    leader, people   ☐   ☐   ☐   ☐
    tend to follow me.

14. I am impatient.   ☐   ☐   ☐   ☐

15. I am rebellious.   ☐   ☐   ☐   ☐

16. I am a strategic
    thinker.   ☐   ☐   ☐   ☐

17. I am a creative
    problem solver.   ☐   ☐   ☐   ☐

18. I immediately
    blame myself
    when something   ☐   ☐   ☐   ☐
    goes wrong.

19. I get bored easily.   ☐   ☐   ☐   ☐

20. I always see the
       big picture.   ☐   ☐   ☐   ☐

21. I have street
       smarts and com-   ☐   ☐   ☐   ☐
       mon sense.

22. I am comfortable
       taking risks.   ☐   ☐   ☐   ☐

23. I am very
       independent.   ☐   ☐   ☐   ☐

24. I am optimistic.   ☐   ☐   ☐   ☐

25. If I fail, I try
       again.   ☐   ☐   ☐   ☐

Total number of each
ranking   ☐   ☐   ☐   ☐

                 x1   x2   x3   x4

Multiply by the
number above   ☐   ☐   ☐   ☐

Add all four numbers to determine the percentage score that reflects the
probability that you're an entrepreneur-in-the-making: [%]

Again, this isn't a pass/fail test. It's an assessment. The
higher you score, the more likely that you're an entrepreneur-
in-the-making. A good rule of thumb is a score of 90 percent

probability or higher. Also, remember the entrepreneurial range. A lower score might mean being self-employed is still a strong option for you; it may just be in more of a lifestyle business.

You can download the Entrepreneur-in-the-Making Assessment or fill it out online at e-leap.com.

You can find other great assessment/profiling tools that can help you continue to validate that you have some of the fundamental entrepreneurial traits.

One tool to determine if you have some of these entrepreneurial characteristics is the Kolbe A™ Index. This profiling tool helps you understand in which of four modes you naturally put your instinctive energy: (1) Fact Finder, (2) Follow Thru, (3) Quick Start, and (4) Implementor. It gives you a score of one to ten in each of these areas, ten being highest. For the sake of this book, we'll focus only on the Quick Start mode. Entrepreneurs tend to be "high Quick Starts," scoring eight, nine, or ten in this mode.

Amy Bruske, the president of Kolbe Corp, describes a high Quick Start as someone who is innovative, a risk taker, and a change agent. High Quick Starts improvise, ad lib, and experiment through trial and error, being willing to fail if necessary. They have mind-sets that look toward the future, and want to create change for change's sake. In our conversation, Amy said that a person seven or higher in Quick Start "creates things that don't currently exist or makes major changes to what does."

You can learn more about the Kolbe A™ Index by going to Kolbe.com/a.

Another profiling tool is called Culture Index, and it's a bit more complex than the Kolbe A(TM) Index. Culture Index, Inc., cofounded by Gary W. Walstrom, measures seven different work-related traits. They're labeled A through D, EU, L, and I. For the sake of this book, we are going to focus on only the A and C traits.

In each trait, you fall into a range of "sigmas," ranging from 1–6. The higher your A trait and the lower your C trait, the more likely you have some of the characteristics of an entrepreneur-in-the-making. Incidentally, my A trait is in the sixth sigma, and my C trait is in the first sigma.

Jason Williford, managing licensee of Culture Index Dallas/ Ft. Worth, explains the higher your A trait, the more dominantly proactive you are and the lower your C trait, the more you lack patience. The combination of these two traits creates a forward drive in a person that must move quickly.

He explains that if you don't have these traits, no matter how hard you work, you'll lack the risk tolerance, relentless pursuit, and drive to succeed. You can learn more about the Culture Index Program by going to cultureindex.com or contacting Jason Williford at jwilliford@cultureindex.com.

SUMMARY

At this point, I hope that you have a determination with absolute clarity. Either you have all of the traits of an entrepreneur, or you don't. If not, I hope I've convinced you not to take an entrepreneurial leap.

If this is the case, I genuinely hope you find the clarity freeing and validating. Finding your true calling is a process of elimination, and you're now one step closer to knowing what yours is.

I would also suggest that if the entrepreneurial spirit appeals to you but you don't have all of the characteristics, you might consider joining forces and partnering with an entrepreneur. They always need to be counterbalanced by an "Integrator," someone who fills an equally vital role in growing an organization.

An Integrator is someone who helps an entrepreneur run the day-to-day affairs of the business and execute the plan. This vital role is also known as COO, Number Two, or Right-Hand Person. For more information on becoming an Integrator, read my book, with coauthor Mark C. Winters, *Rocket Fuel: The One Essential Combination That Will Get You More of What You Want from Your Business*. In addition to teaching entrepreneurs how to get to the next level, *Rocket Fuel* also explains the powerful Visionary/Integrator dynamic that makes most companies successful, along with teaching Integrators how to be great at their job.

For everyone else, if you're now convinced—despite all the conditions and requirements I've explained—that you're an entrepreneur-in-the-making, let's get to work. The next step—part II—is showing you a glimpse of what your life as an entrepreneur could look like.

PART II

GLIMPSE

Part II is intended to provide a glimpse of what your life could look like if you pursue your natural entrepreneurial abilities and gifts. Once you know what's possible, you can better choose where and how far you want to go.

I want to point out first that there are many more entrepreneurial options than just the Silicon Valley, billion-dollar tech companies that get most of the press. You have hundreds of industries to choose from when taking the entrepreneurial leap, as well as thousands of products and services you can create or improve, along with choices of how big a business you really want to build.

The billion-dollar tech companies are the one-in-a-million stories, and besides, they aren't all they're cracked up to be. In most cases, they aren't for you. You might be much happier with a closet-renovating business generating $4 million in revenue and $1 million in profit—a company that's the best in your industry, where your employees are happy, and you and they are making lots of money.

Jim Collins, the business author of *Good to Great,* says, "The greatest company in America we'll never know, because it's some $10 million company in middle America that doesn't want to be known." This quote motivated me, as I wanted to build that exact company, and I feel we did. As we built EOS Worldwide, we had no desire to be on any "fastest-growing" or "best places to work" lists. Although we would have ranked very high on them if we'd pursued the claim, it just wasn't important to us. We were more focused on being a great company that was the best for our clients. When we decided to sell, we had over fifty interested buyers.

I point this out to show you that entrepreneurs flourish on all sorts of levels. By the end of part II, you'll be able to decide what's most important to you. To be the biggest, the best, the most recognized, or the most charitable; a million-dollar company, $10 million company, $100 million company, or a billion-dollar company. There's no right or wrong answer, only the answer that's best for you. True entrepreneurs don't follow the herd or care about what everyone else thinks.

In part II, you'll also get a good glimpse of what your day-to-day life can look like, both the bright and dark sides of the entrepreneur's life, along with real-life stories of entrepreneurs and their journeys with different types of industries, businesses, and business sizes, to help you discover which appeal most to you. These real-life examples can also help you start clarifying your own vision.

You'll see both the dream scenario—the freedom and creativity that are possible—and the nightmare scenario—the setbacks, struggles, and mistakes. My hope is that reading about the potential nightmares will help you avoid many of them.

The goal is to give you a glimpse of your future as an entrepreneur and motivate you to get going. At the end of each chapter, while your thoughts are fresh in your mind, a worksheet has been provided to capture your insights, ideas, and decisions.

Here's your Glimpse.

CHAPTER 6

BUSINESSES, INDUSTRIES, AND SIZES

The objective of this chapter is to show all of your options for creating a business. Whether you want to create a $50 million heating-and-cooling company with a hundred employees that focuses on residential customers, a $500,000 marketing firm with five employees whose clients are companies that focus on selling products to women, or the next publicly held billion-dollar unicorn tech company with tens of thousands of employees. These and many other options are all available to you.

What's most important to determine is which options you're most drawn to. Three main factors will determine the business you ultimately choose:

1. Industry
2. Type of business
3. Size of business

As you read about each of these factors, I hope you'll have a light bulb moment about what appeals most to you. The idea is to find a concept that fits with your passions and genetic code.

My passion, for example, is teaching. I love turning the light bulb on for people. My previous two businesses—both training companies—were in the education industry. I also prefer to run small companies. The first had about fifty people, my second around two hundred total. That's my sweet spot. I have no passion for, on one end, a thousand-person company or, at the other end, a one-person show. One of the reasons I sold the second business was that it was getting bigger than what I enjoy.

In addition to being in the education industry, I also prefer selling services, so I lean toward service businesses. I have no real interest in product businesses. These are all qualifications that you'll need to decide for yourself. As you place filters on what you envision, the picture of what you truly want will become clearer.

Let's take each of the major factors—industry, type of business, and size of business—and break them down one at a time.

FIRST FACTOR: INDUSTRY

An internet search of *industries* will produce a list of hundreds of industries available to you. To expand the scope of your imagination, go ahead and do a search first. And to get your gears turning, below is a list of about fifty industries that I've worked with. Simply glancing over them will give you a sense of all the possibilities available to you.

INDUSTRIES

Accounting	Legal
Agriculture	Logistics
Architectural/Engineering	Manufacturing/Fabrication
Asphalt/Paving	Mechanical
Auto Dealer	Medical/Dental/Chiropractic
Auto Repair	Mortgage Company
Cell Phone Retailer	Nonprofits
Concrete	Online Retail
Contracting	Pest Control
Conveyors/Belting	Physical Therapy
Database Security	Plumbing
Diamond Brokerage	PR/Marketing
Distribution (hat & glove, ball bearing, beverage, food, etc.)	Printing
Electrical	Real Estate Brokerage
Equipment Dealer	Real Estate Property Management
Event Planning	Real Estate Title Services
Financial Services	Restaurants
Gen. Contractor/Construction	Retail Service Providers
Hearing Clinics	Retirement Plans
Heating and Cooling (HVAC)	Software Development
Home & Business Security	Sports Facilities
Hotels	Staffing
Insurance Agency	Third-Party Administrator (TPA)
IT (Information Technology)	Trucking
Landscaping	Web Application Developer

As you can see, you can choose from many more options than just tech companies. In fact, most aren't high tech, although you may decide to apply high-tech innovations to them.

Now that you have the context of *industry*, let's go a level deeper because, within each industry, there are many different types of businesses.

SECOND FACTOR: TYPE OF BUSINESS

Within each industry, "type of business" is defined by three different aspects:

1. Service or product
2. B2B (business-to-business) or B2C (business-to-consumer)
3. High end or low cost

Let's consider them one at a time.

1. Service or Product

First, you need to decide whether you're drawn to the service side or the product side. To explain the differences between these two types of companies, let's start with service businesses. These firms typically charge a fee for the work that's performed. For instance, attorneys and accountants charge an hourly rate, a landscaping company charges you each time they cut your lawn, and a marketing firm charges you a flat monthly rate to build your brand and increase your social-media presence. Service businesses basically sell the owner's or employees' time.

Examples of service companies include auto repair, IT services, project management, event planning, financial planning, medical practices, logistics, mortgage brokers, home cleaning, physical therapy, software development, architecture, hair salons, and spas.

On the other hand, product businesses make, sell, or distribute tangible products. That may be appealing to you, as many entrepreneurs like to touch, feel, and see what their business sells. It's hard to do that with a service, because you're selling an intangible. Many people prefer tangibles. If this describes you, then you're probably more drawn to a product business.

Product businesses include agriculture, auto dealerships, retail stores, and companies that manufacture things, such as equipment, food, supplements, tires, watches, metal fabrications, or textiles. You can also choose among product distribution companies that distribute products, such as food, beverage, clothing, raw materials, furniture, and computers.

Some companies include both products and services. For example, construction companies provide both general contracting as a service *and* the building they construct, which is a product. Another example is a software company that sells accounting software, which is a product, *and* also provides a service to implement and support the product. A commercial heating-and-cooling (HVAC) contractor sells their customer both a $25,000 air conditioning unit for their building, which is a product, *and* a contract for a fee to maintain it, which is a service.

An example of a company that combines both is image-One, a company founded by entrepreneurs Rob Dube and Joel Pearlman. The duo started their entrepreneurial careers by selling Blow Pops out of their lockers in ninth grade. After graduating college, they recognized a need in the printer industry for remanufactured toner cartridges. Their company now provides both a service—simplifying their corporate customers' printing environments—and a product—printing equipment. Of their $18 million in revenue, 75 percent comes from the service side, and 25 percent comes from products.

2. B2B or B2C

The second aspect of choosing a type of business is deciding between B2B (business-to-business) or B2C (business-to-consumer). In other words, whether you choose a product or service business, you can sell to two types of customers, businesses or consumers. B2B companies sell services or products to other businesses. B2C companies sell directly to consumers: individuals or families.

Ultimately, you have to decide if you're more passionate about working with businesses or consumers. I personally prefer selling to businesses, while a good entrepreneur friend of mine prefers selling to consumers. As an example, certain construction companies only build commercial buildings for businesses, and other construction companies only build homes for consumers. Some software companies develop apps for businesses, and others develop apps for consumers. When Verizon sells a hundred cell phones to a corporation, they're B2B. When they sell one cell phone to a customer, they're B2C.

Which do you prefer? Selling to consumers or businesses?

3. High End or Low Cost

Going another level deeper, the third aspect of business is high end or low cost. You need to decide if the product or service you offer will be high quality/high price, and typically lower volume, or lower quality/low price, and typically higher volume. Where do your passions lie? Deciding is important, because it's extremely difficult and rare to succeed at offering both.

In everything I've ever done, my only option is to provide the highest quality at the highest price. I always want to provide a premium service. It's how I'm wired, and that helps direct me to the types of businesses I'm interested in starting.

At the same time, I have clients who offer the lowest-priced product in their industry. Their customers love them, and they're wildly successful and very passionate about what they do. There's no wrong answer when choosing between these two options.

There's only the best answer for you and your company. What are you drawn to?

For instance, two leading companies, Walmart and Nordstrom, appeal to very different consumers. Some successful car companies sell economy cars without all the bells and whistles, and others achieve success by selling luxury cars with all of the accessories you could ever want.

Here's a template to help give you a context for the difference between the two types of businesses. Let's look at the automobile industry example:

	Economy Car Dealership	Luxury Car Dealership
Industry	Automobile	Automobile
Product or Service	Product	Product
B2B or B2C	B2C	B2C
High End or Low Cost	Low Cost	High End

Let's look at another example: event planning. Certain event-planning companies specialize in high-exposure, premier corporate events, like the Super Bowl and the Academy Awards, and others specialize in everyday, business-as-usual corporate meetings. The high-end event-planning company charges a huge premium for their services, because they're known as the best in the business. The everyday corporate event-planning company, which offers the best price, is also highly successful.

	Everyday Corporate Event Planning	High Exposure, Premier Event Planning
Industry	Event Planning	Event Planning
Product or Service	Service	Service
B2B or B2C	B2B	B2B
High End or Low Cost	Low Cost	High End

I don't expect you to come up with that answer right now—although maybe you already have! The goal is to provide you with a context that will help you arrive at an answer. To recap the context:

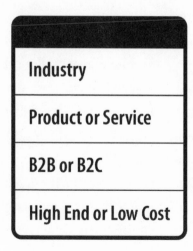

It's important that this context is clear to you before we move on. If not, please review what you've read so far in this chapter. Assuming this is clear, let's move to the final option for the business you want to build: size.

THIRD FACTOR: SIZE OF BUSINESS

The final factor, size, is vital. You must know what you're built for. Are you shooting for a million-dollar company, a billion-dollar company, or something in between? It might seem strange to be thinking about how big a company you want to build when you haven't even started your business and don't even know what type of business you're going to start. Please suspend any disbelief, because I've learned that if you can begin your entrepreneurial journey with the end in mind, you'll get there faster and avoid a lot of frustration. You'll make better decisions and avoid many of the mistakes you don't need to make.

Top-line annual revenue ($1 million, $10 million, $100 million) will be used as the gauge of size. Revenue is used as the gauge because it's the most widely recognized measure of a company's size. Bottom-line profits and number of employees are also important measures, and those will be addressed later.

All of the media hype about billion-dollar companies has almost every entrepreneur-in-the-making wanting to build a company that size. I beg you to reconsider. Building a billion-dollar company is not the fantasy portrayed in the press, and most entrepreneurs aren't equipped to start and build a billion-dollar company every step of the way. The person capable of pulling it off is truly one in a million. Not only that, but also if you could somehow mentally put yourself in the actual CEO seat, at the helm of the billion-dollar company that you think you want ten years from now, most of you would likely say, "Holy shit, I don't want that life!"

In Detroit, there's an amazing entrepreneur billionaire, Dan Gilbert, who built Quicken Loans and owns over a hundred properties in the downtown area. He's helped turn the city around. I have many clients who want to get to Dan Gilbert's level and compare themselves to him. My response is always, "With all due respect, you aren't Dan Gilbert." They have no idea what it's like, to live the life he had to, to build what he has built. The press, the competition, the personal sacrifices, the complexity, the demands, the microscope you're always under—it's all magnified greatly at that level. I know I couldn't have done it, and most entrepreneurs couldn't either.

You don't have to shoot that high. A friend of mine is great at building and selling $10 million companies. He's done it twice and is now on his third one. He tried to build a $100 million company once, and it failed. I told him, "I think your genetic code is building $10 million companies." He looked back and realized that was true, and it's what he's done ever since. You can make a huge impact, become very wealthy, and help a lot of people by building $10 million companies.

You can take any type of business and build it to whatever size you choose. You can build a house-cleaning company to anywhere from $100,000 to $1 billion. You can build a million-dollar used-car dealership, or a billion-dollar network of car dealerships. You can build a software company that does $5 million, $50 million, or $500 million in revenue. The beauty is that you get to decide.

Let's take an example: pretend you're passionate about creating a high-end makeup line. Adding up the factors, you have chosen to be in the cosmetics industry, where you plan to sell a product to consumers, which will be high end.

	Make-Up Business
Industry	Cosmetics
Product or Service	Product
B2B or B2C	B2C
High End or Low Cost	High End

Now pretend your cosmetics line is wildly successful. Now you must decide how big you want your company to become.

Some entrepreneurs would be very happy with a small, boutique business that sells a wonderful high-end makeup line online to a select set of customers—generating $2 million a year, employing only five employees, bringing in high profits, and you, as the owner, are having a great time at work every day.

Another entrepreneur might take the exact same product and create a $500 million company with their product in every high-end retail store, a huge online retail presence, and a world-wide brand. This company would also be highly profitable, with 1,500 employees and an empire to manage.

As you can see, the exact same product, two totally different businesses to manage. Which appeals to you? How do you want to be spending your time ten years from now?

Most entrepreneurs wouldn't be able to grow that business to $500 million, nor should they, because they don't have the passion or interest for a company of that size. You might decide to keep revenues at $2 million or sell the company for many millions of dollars once it hits $5 or $10 million in annual revenue. Again, you should decide what's right for you.

Another factor to consider here is your company's annual earnings. While we've been using top-line revenue to determine business size, revenue is essentially irrelevant when you take ego and outside forces (the public, the press, shareholders, competitors) out of the equation. What truly matters is profit. Some $10 million companies generate a 20 percent profit. That's $2 million. Some $100 million companies generate a 2 percent profit. That's also $2 million.

The $10 million company, generating a $2 million profit, with fewer employees and transactions, has less complexity. It puts the exact same amount of profit in your pocket as the owner, with a lot fewer headaches. For most entrepreneurs, this is a better scenario.

You might find it interesting to know that, at the time of this writing, Apple generated about a 22 percent profit. And Walmart has historically generated less than a 3 percent profit (as most retailers do). And incidentally, at the time we sold EOS Worldwide, we were generating about a 50 percent profit. You'll find the average company profit benchmark to be about 10 percent, but every industry is different, as you can see.

In addition, the number of employees is as important as profitability. Some entrepreneurs only want five employees, and some are comfortable with a hundred thousand. Yours might be ten, or it might be a thousand. Companies become increasingly more complex as they reach certain employee-size stages—for instance, ten, fifty, two hundred and fifty, and a thousand employees. Each one of those employee sizes creates a new level of regulations and demands on you to oversee the operation. You really need to give this some thought. How many people do you want to be responsible for?

Let's review the factors to determine what kind of business you want:

1. Industry
2. Type of business (service or product, B2B or B2C, high end or low cost)
3. Size of business

If you're still not sure what's right for you, that's normal at this point. Again, what's vital is that you understand the overall context. Knowing that will frame your thinking as you read on and as you learn about and see many different businesses.

The following is an exercise that might help you decide what business is right for you. Think about the type of people you like to work with, serve, help, and be around. Knowing this will help you clarify the business, because you'll be clearer about the type of customers or clients you'll be selling to.

For example, after a conversation with one entrepreneur-in-the-making, I came away impressed for two reasons. One was that he knew he wanted to sell services to consumers in their homes (among them, HVAC, plumbing, blinds installation, painting, carpet installation, appliance repair, roofing, etc.) Number two, it's rare for someone in their midtwenties to be passionate about those types of industries. That creates a huge opportunity for him, as the entrepreneurs in those industries are getting older, which creates a huge void. Knowing that he likes selling services and products to in-home consumers will really help him narrow the field of what business he's going to start.

That example points out another factor that can be used to narrow down your choice.

Who do you enjoy serving? It might be a client base of ultrawealthy people. So you start a jet-cleaning business, a chauffeur service, or a yacht-building company. You might love working with mothers of young children, so you create products and services to make their lives better. You might love beer-drinking, sports-loving thirty-year-olds, so you open a chain of craft-beer sports bars or an apparel business that sells them their favorite T-shirts.

I love entrepreneurs, and I'm going to spend my life serving them and solving their problems. It gives me great joy helping them realize total freedom. Therefore, the businesses and services I come up with will always serve entrepreneurs. Knowing this helps me zero in on the business that is right for me.

As Dan Sullivan puts it, "Who do you want to be a hero to?"

SUMMARY

When you weigh the different factors presented in this chapter, the possibilities for which business to choose are endless. If you're an entrepreneur-in-the-making, you'll discover the one that is right for you.

For some assistance in helping you pin down the right industry, business, and company size for you, go to e-leap.com and use the MyBiz Match tool.

If you aren't sure, you just need to try a lot of stuff. When I was twenty-one, I thought I wanted to start a corporate travel agency. So I went to work for one. I discovered within a few months that I absolutely hated the travel business. It was low margin and highly competitive. I should add that while it wasn't the business for me, it suits others just fine. The owner of the company I worked for had built it up into a $10 million corporate travel agency, loved operating it, and on top of that, he was revered in the industry. You too can experiment. Test-drive a business to find out how passionate you really are about it.

At this point, we've confirmed you're an entrepreneur-in-the-making, and you now know the many kinds of businesses available to you. The next chapter will provide some real-life examples of what entrepreneurs did to reach where they are now. Of course, they started out just like you, as entrepreneurs-in-the-making.

Before we move on, please take a minute to write down any thoughts and ideas this chapter prompted for you. Write down the industries that appeal to you, the types of businesses—service or product, B2B or B2C, high end or low cost—and the size of the business, as well as any other additional thoughts you may have.

WORKSHEET

What Appeals to You?

Industries	
Product or Service	
B2B or B2C	
High End or Low Cost	
Size of Business	

Additional Thoughts

_____

_____

_____

_____

_____

_____

_____

_____

_____

_____

_____

_____

_____

_____

What action can you take in the next seven days to help you decide what business is right for you?

You can download MyBiz Match and all
worksheets and tools at e-leap.com.

Chapter 7

Real-Life Entrepreneurial Stories

There are thousands of amazing stories about entrepreneurs starting and building their businesses. I highly recommend that you read as many as you can. They will give you incredible insights and inspiration to take your leap. Along with the following list I will provide you in the chapter, a quick internet search of "entrepreneurial success stories" and the list of resources at the end of this book will give you many more.

FAMOUS ENTREPRENEURS

You probably already know some of the stories about big-name entrepreneurs who started and built business empires. Here are a few that show the upper end of what an entrepreneur can create:

Steve Jobs cofounded Apple with Steve Wozniak to sell Wozniak's Apple I Computer. He went door-to-door looking for a retailer to sell their computers. They made their first sale when the owner of a computer store in the San Francisco Bay area ordered fifty. This is how the Apple empire started, a company in the computer industry that expanded into phones, music, and apps and became the first company worth more than one trillion dollars.

In an earlier era, Henry Ford democratized the automobile, failing multiple times before finally starting the Ford Motor Company and creating a car—the Model T—that appealed to the masses. Ford Motor Company is still going strong over a hundred years later, a multibillion-dollar company and one of the largest automobile manufacturers in the world.

Walt Disney cofounded the Walt Disney Company with his brother Roy in the 1920s. Walt started as an innovative cartoonist who eventually created the cartoon character Mickey Mouse. He began creating and distributing animated short films and then animated feature-length films. He added live-action motion pictures, TV shows, and theme parks to ultimately build the Disney empire.

In 1994, Jeff Bezos started an online bookstore in his garage. He built it to become the largest online retailer in the world. He became the world's wealthiest person in 2017 when his net worth exceeded $90 billion.

LESS-FAMOUS SUCCESSFUL ENTREPRENEURS

Those big-name entrepreneurs are one in a million, though. You might be just as encouraged by the huge crowd of lesser-known entrepreneurs who are incredibly successful, wealthy, and happy. They chose not to build multibillion-dollar public companies, but still make a huge impact on their employees, families, and communities.

Here are eight of those lesser-known stories:

Story One: Sam Simon's energy-distribution company, Atlas Oil, does $1 billion in revenue and has a thousand employees.

Sam and his family moved to America from Iraq with no money and owing $200 to their church. They lived in the basement of Sam's dad's best friend, who owned a gas station. Sam, his dad, and his brothers all worked at the gas station.

Before long, they noticed the owner wasn't making maximum use of the ice machine in the gas station, so Sam's dad made his friend an offer to sell the ice and split the profits fifty-fifty.

Sam, his dad, and his brothers quickly grew the ice business to the second largest ice distributor in the state, distributing ice to bars, party stores, gas stations, drugstores, and marinas. They then sold the business. They also took over running a gas station that was closed. Once they turned it around, they started buying other gas stations. They grew that business to forty gas stations.

At age sixteen, Sam had twenty-two employees who reported directly to him.

Then Sam saw a huge opportunity present itself in the fuel-distribution business. He left the family business when he was in his early twenties and started Atlas Oil Company to distribute fuel to gas stations. In the last thirty-five years, he has bought and sold over six hundred gas stations and has built his energy-distribution company to the $1 billion company that it is today.

Story Two: By the time Francy Lucido of Michigan Staffing and Aspen Search Group was twenty-six, she was creating, managing, and conducting training programs for economically disadvantaged youth and single moms.

Her father, Frank Lucido, was a successful manufacturers rep in the automotive industry when one of his clients offered him an opportunity to become a sales rep for their staffing needs. Frank, seeing a great business opportunity, approached his daughter Francy, who he knew had the entrepreneurial gene.

"Do you want to try this?" he asked, and after some research, they jumped into the staffing business and became partners. Frank's brainchild was born. He financially backed the endeavor and provided Francy mentorship and advice; the rest is history.

Francy built the firm to a $20 million company, diversifying out of the automotive industry and focusing on placing administrative, light industrial, and technical workers in multiple industries. Her mom (who managed finances for the company before retiring) and dad are still partners in the business, along with Francy's sister, who is the CFO.

Story Three: Todd Sachse of Sachse Construction started his story by saying, "You are either wired to be an entrepreneur or you aren't; it's in your chromosomes."

When Todd was twelve years old, in seventh grade, he would ride his bike two miles to a candy store, where he bought Fireballs for three cents apiece, and then sold them to his fellow students for twenty-five cents. He said, "The margins were great."

He also had a pottery/ceramic business that sold pottery to stores and gave pottery lessons to school kids paid for by their parents.

At age sixteen, Todd and a friend took over his brother's small window-washing business and grew it all through college.

He also started a maid service in his junior year of college and continued to grow both businesses. In his senior year of pre-med, as he was about to go off to medical school, he called his mom to inform her that he "wasn't going to medical school and was instead going to wash windows and clean toilets."

He continued to grow both businesses until he sold them at age twenty-eight. He let them go because he had become enamored with real estate and construction. That's because he began buying and renovating real estate starting at age twenty-four.

After he and a friend bought a ten-acre piece of land and built a hundred-unit apartment building, he was hooked. He went fully into the construction business, starting with a $25,000 line of credit from his bank and calling everyone he knew to find anyone who would let him build them a building.

Twenty-seven years later, Sachse Construction is a $175 million construction company with 165 employees. Todd also owns four other companies, and his five companies combined employ over three hundred people.

Story Four: Mike Nehra, of Vintage King Audio, was a rock musician. He moved to New York City at age twenty-one to join a band with a recording contract.

He found that New York was expensive and the money he was making in the band wasn't enough to live on. In his search to make extra money, he realized he had a knack for buying and selling high-end recording studio equipment for a nice profit.

He would find equipment advertised for sale in *The Village Voice* that was undervalued, buy it, and then with a gift for word-smithing, would advertise and sell the exact same equipment in the *Village Voice* a few days later. At twenty-five, he moved back to his home city to join a band with his brother that had a recording contract with RCA, Robert Bradley's Blackwater Surprise. They released two successful albums and toured successfully for years.

While on the road, Mike continued to sell equipment from his cell phone at truck stops. With the success of his equipment sales, he and his brother, Andrew, started Vintage King Audio. They realized that the exchange rates in Europe were so good that they could buy equipment overseas on credit cards for half the price they could sell them for in the United States.

They made good profits doing this while touring, until Mike turned forty and he and Andrew decided to get off the road and make a full-time commitment to Vintage King Audio. Twelve years later, Mike and Andrew have built it into a $50 million company with ninety-five employees.

Story Five: Steven Carse was working as an analyst at AIG when the great recession of 2008 hit, and unfortunately, due to layoffs, he lost his job.

With $7,000 in savings and a passion for popsicles, he took his entrepreneurial leap. He wanted to open a retail brick-and-mortar location but realized it was far too expensive, so he bought $6,000 in equipment and started selling frozen treats out of a pushcart at a gas station. He quickly created a raving fan base and decided to grow the business.

At the time Steven's brother, Nick, who had a secure job as an attorney, was helping Steven on nights and weekends making pops. Steven asked Nick to join him full-time. They became fifty-fifty partners, and their company, King of Pops, was born. They sold uniquely flavored pops (e.g., chocolate sea salt, raspberry lime, cookies 'n' cream, banana puddin') out of carts in parks, at parties, farmers markets, and so on. The business continued to grow. They hired friends to help them as they did everything they could to meet demand.

Eight years later, King of Pops now has over a hundred carts and sells its products online and through retail channels such as Whole Foods and in sports stadiums. They have expanded to eight cities with 60 full-time and 350 part-time employees in their peak season and generate $9 million a year in revenue.

Story Six: Necole Parker-Green, founder, principal, and CEO of The ELOCEN Group, worked for a government contractor that managed a range of program- and project-management government contracts. At the age of thirty-six, she was generating 70 percent of the company's revenue, but after a performance review meeting that didn't go well, she became fed up with the way she was being treated and decided to quit. The next day, she handed her employer two letters—a letter of resignation and a letter of consultancy, offering to serve as a consultant for the company. Although caught off guard, her employer accepted the deal. Simultaneously, she started her own program- and project-management business within the construction industry. Because of her integrity, Necole told her former employer that as a consultant, she wouldn't take away any existing deals, but anything new she turned up was fair game.

Over the next eleven years, Necole built a successful business, generating over $100 million in revenues, employing a team of fifty professionals, and having three of her previous large employers becoming subcontractors of hers. Her achievements have also included receiving the US Small Business Administration's highest entrepreneurial Small Business Person of the Year award and numerous other commendations for her success as a female in the predominantly male construction industry.

Story Seven: Shawn Stafford grew up in a tough part of Detroit, Michigan. He found himself going down the wrong path when, in eighth grade, three life-changing events happened to him: He was robbed at gunpoint, one of his friends went to prison, and another was murdered.

He was failing school, and his mom, whom he respected very much, saw the road he was on and said to him, "I thought you were a leader?" These words stuck with him, and he decided from that day forward he was going to lead and not follow.

In eleventh grade, a teacher took an interest in him and inspired him to go to college. He worked hard and was accepted into Michigan State University.

After graduating college, he got a corporate job working at Chrysler and then Ford Motor Company. His job enabled him to travel the world and make a six-figure income. While working at Ford, he read Napoleon Hill's book, *Think and Grow Rich*, and Robert T. Kiyosaki's book, *Rich Dad, Poor Dad: What the Rich Teach Their Kids About Money—That the Poor and Middle Class Do Not!* These two books gave him his light bulb moment, and he decided he didn't want to work for someone for the rest of his life. He began buying rental properties on credit cards. Once he started to reach a level of success, his boss became aware of what he was doing and forced his hand.

He left Ford Motor Company to take his entrepreneurial leap

as a real estate investor. He began buying apartment buildings, networking and building a name for himself, and today, at age forty-six, he owns just under five thousand apartment units and has 120 employees, and his commercial real estate company generates $50 million a year in revenue.

Story Eight: Not all entrepreneurs make revolutionary discoveries. Starting a great company can involve no more than besting your competition. Joe Haney, for instance, had always wanted to be an entrepreneur by the age of thirty. I shared Joe's story about clearing the fallen concrete wall for his dad earlier in this book. At the age of twenty-nine, he was working in a car dealership as the finance and insurance manager when he learned that the owner of the dealership wanted to bring more services in-house to provide a "complete solution" for their customers. This endeavor would entail a strategic alliance with an insurance company and other vendors.

Joe agreed to take on the project and assemble the strategic alliances. When meeting with potential insurance companies, Joe was unimpressed and had a light bulb moment. He would start his own insurance agency.

He spent months putting together his vision and worked tirelessly to find an insurance carrier to underwrite his company. After finding a carrier, he convinced the dealership to make *him* their insurance company. He quickly added more carriers and clients, and two years later, he added a fifty-fifty partner, Paul Mattes. Together they have built Sterling Insurance Group into one of the top ten largest agencies in their state and top two hundred nationwide out of thirty-nine thousand insurance brokers.

These not-so-well-known entrepreneurs may not get the accolades their better-known, multibillion-dollar peers receive, but that doesn't make them any less successful or happy. In every case, big name or not, the story is the same. An entrepreneur-in-the-making, like you, with the six essential traits, sees an opportunity and takes the leap. Whether you want to be a high-profile or low-profile entrepreneur is your choice. Either way, you're a success.

SUMMARY

None of the above stories include the obstacles, barriers, and failures these entrepreneurs experienced. Getting your ass kicked is also part of the process, and every one of these entrepreneurs has experienced many setbacks. There aren't enough pages to list every issue those entrepreneurs faced, nor is it necessary. Because the point of this chapter was to show you examples of what's possible. Once you lock on to your idea, your six essential traits—your vision, passion, problem-solving, drive, risk-taking, and sense of responsibility—will come into play, and you'll overcome whatever is thrown at you.

These entrepreneurs had to make literally hundreds of course corrections, as well as thousands of minor decisions, for their businesses to succeed. There's no playbook for how to solve these issues, because every product, service, competitor, and customer is unique. If you have passion for your product or service and obsess about what your customer needs, the answers will come in the heat of the crisis.

Anyone who tries to tell you there's a universal solution to every business issue is lying. There are hundreds of possible solutions to setbacks or specific problems in business when you take into account the industry, type of business, specific product or service, level of quality, type of customer, vision, plan, core values, growth trajectory, and the specific issue you're facing. If you're fully engaged and have the six traits, the right solution will appear.

Before we go on to take a look at a day in the life of an entrepreneur, please take a few minutes to write down what you learned in this chapter. I urge you to focus on what excites, what scares, and what inspires you. Just write exactly what you're thinking right now. What can you improve on, or what doesn't yet exist?

WORKSHEET

_____

_____

_____

_____

_____

_____

_____

_____

_____

_____

_____

_____

_____

_____

_____

_____

_____

_____

_____

_____

_____

_____

What action does this chapter inspire you to take in the next seven days that will help you get closer to taking your entrepreneurial leap?

_____

_____

_____

_____

_____

_____

_____

_____

_____

_____

_____

_____

_____

_____

_____

_____

_____

_____

_____

You can download all worksheets and tools at

e-leap.com.

CHAPTER 8

LIVING THE DREAM: A DAY IN THE LIFE

The objective in the next two chapters is to create a vivid picture. Once you see the best-case and worst-case scenarios, you'll be better able to avoid mistakes and get where you want to go faster. All kinds of things happen, both good and bad, when people take the entrepreneurial leap. In your case, better to know now rather than later.

First, you'll see a dream picture of what life could look like. It shows what many entrepreneurs' lives in fact look like. The next chapter will show you the nightmare, what other entrepreneurs' lives look like. The contrast will be obvious, and you'll clearly see why you want to end up closer to the dream end of the spectrum.

DREAM ├─────────┤ NIGHTMARE

THE DREAM

This scenario is possible. I help my clients achieve it every day. However, it's possible only after you take the leap (which we'll cover in chapter 14) and survive the start-up phase (which we'll cover in chapter 15). The dream is the reward for the tough years of building your business.

For this exercise to be most effective, you need to put yourself into the following scenario. Picture this. It's ten years from now. Your offering to the world has taken off. Your clients or customers love and appreciate it. You have great people working for you, who are as passionate about your product or service as you are. They're as passionate about your customers as you are. They work hard and are fully engaged every day. Everyone is crystal clear on their roles and their responsibilities. They're completely accountable and do what they say they will.

You wake up every day at the best time for your unique body, which maximizes your energy. You complete your morning ritual and then head off to work.

At the beginning of each week, you have a meeting with your leadership team, the people who report directly to you. In this meeting, you confirm that all the critical metrics and priorities for the business are on track, and that all your customers and employees are happy. You solve any problems that have arisen and get everything back on track. This sets the tone for the week, and you and your team leave the meeting with clear priorities about what needs to be accomplished over the next seven days to assure that all longer-term goals will be achieved in the coming quarter and year.

You spend time during the week meeting with customers, getting a pulse on their needs, solving their problems, and making sure they're receiving value. You spend planned-out time during the week thinking about and clarifying the company vision and plans. You focus on customer needs and expectations, ideas for innovating, communicating, and delivering your offerings, and ways of staying one step ahead of your competitors.

On average, you solve six problems or make six decisions each day. That's because solving problems and making decisions are responsibilities you'll have until the day you sell your business or retire. You get home at the hour you want, with plenty of time and energy for your family and friends.

As an active business owner, you're juggling about three to five important projects at any given time. Each project is focused on supporting and growing your business, and the process energizes you. It could be a major software implementation, a new offering, an exciting marketing campaign, raising capital, buying a new building, expanding your space, or preparing for a big presentation or big company event.

You pay yourself fairly—an amount equal to the value you provide. This is enough for you to afford your lifestyle and save enough to retire at the age you want.

In addition, you—and your partners (if you have them)—take

a quarterly profit distribution that's above average in your industry, because your company is so well run. Your highly engaged, committed leadership team and employees receive bonuses or profit-sharing for their contribution to generating an above-average bottom line. Your business and its value continue to grow. Every year your business is worth more. Its value is such that if you chose to sell, you'd receive a large amount of money and be financially set.

You also meet with your leadership team every quarter for a full-day planning session to ensure that the company's vision and annual plan are on track, set priorities for the next quarter, and solve all relevant strategic issues. You also meet with your leadership team once a year for a two-day annual planning retreat to set next year's plan, goals, and numbers, and to make sure the team is firing on all cylinders.

During the year, you take as much time off as you choose, which keeps you recharged, balanced, and able to remain a visionary entrepreneur for your people.

Can you see yourself in this dream? That's what can happen when you become a successful entrepreneur. All the cogs of the machine you've created are working in sync.

Now, on to the nightmare end of the spectrum. But before we go there, please capture what you find to be the most appealing aspects of the dream. How do you see your ideal life as an entrepreneur ten years from now? The clearer your vision, the stronger the outcome.

WORKSHEET

_____

_____

_____

_____

_____

_____

_____

_____

_____

_____

_____

_____

_____

_____

_____

_____

_____

_____

_____

_____

_____

What action can you take in the next seven days to assure you'll live the dream scenario?

_____

_____

_____

_____

_____

_____

_____

_____

_____

_____

_____

_____

_____

_____

_____

_____

_____

_____

_____

You can download all worksheets and tools at
e-leap.com.

CHAPTER 9

LIVING THE NIGHTMARE: A DAY IN HELL

So that was the dream scenario some entrepreneurs enjoy. The goal is for you to make that dream scenario come true for you as well. The sad reality, however, is that many entrepreneurs are living a nightmare, the other end of the spectrum. As I share this scenario with you, please realize that this is strictly a cautionary tale. The nightmare scenario is entirely avoidable, and the objective here is to help you avoid it.

THE NIGHTMARE

Here's the nightmare scenario.

Your people aren't engaged, passionate, or concerned about your customers. They show up for their paychecks and can't wait to go home. You spend your time avoiding them, interacting only when absolutely necessary. You meet with your leadership team rarely, and only when there's a crisis to solve. Roles and responsibilities are unclear, and people trip over each other trying to complete projects. When someone says they're going to carry out a task, most of the time they don't.

Your customers and clients are frustrated but stay with you because you offer the lowest price in town. As a result, you barely make a profit, so you're frustrated. Tension is always simmering between you and your customers, and as soon as a better price comes along, they leave without notice. You can only pay yourself enough to survive, and there are no profit distributions.

Since you don't have people you can count on, you're doing half their work, and that means you're forced to work from morning to night and on weekends. You rarely take a vacation and have little to no time for family or friends. Your family is getting fed up because you're never around. When you are, you're always exhausted and frustrated. The stress leads to bad decisions and poor health. You have high turnover, and you have to constantly train new employees. They don't respect you, and they might steal from you, treat your clients poorly, and ultimately damage your brand. These businesses struggle until their founders ultimately burn out and the business dies or is acquired by a competitor for pennies on the dollar.

Sound like fun?

This nightmare can be avoided. I help entrepreneurs do it every day.

EIGHT CRITICAL MISTAKES THAT CREATE THE NIGHTMARE SCENARIO

What are the mistakes to avoid if you want to live the dream rather than the nightmare? First off, you have to assume that you'll make mistakes. Everyone does. Here's a list of the crucial ones, so you'll burn them in your subconscious. That way you can take steps to avoid them.

1. Not Having a Vision

It's vital to have a crystal clear vision of where the company is going and to share that vision with your people often so that they see the vision as clearly as you do.

2. Hiring the Wrong People

When hiring anyone, you must confirm that they have your company's core values. Hire slowly. If, unfortunately, you hire the wrong person, you have to be willing to fire quickly. Whenever you hire, always think long term. Don't hire to solve a short-term problem.

3. Not Spending Time with Your People

It's critical that you stay in sync with your people. This means meeting with them weekly, quarterly, and annually. Keep them in the loop about everything that's going on. Give them feedback on how they're doing, and make sure they know they can give you feedback on how you're doing as well. Solve interpersonal issues quickly so everyone is rowing in the same direction.

4. Not Knowing Who Your Customer Is

As early in the process of taking your entrepreneurial leap as possible, you should determine the exact demographics and psychographics of your ideal customer. This is knowing exactly who they are, where they are, and what they are. You'll then avoid taking a buckshot approach to marketing and falling into the trap of trying to please everyone. You want to make sure you clearly know your customer so that you can speak their language in all of your marketing and sales efforts.

5. Not Charging Enough

It's extremely common for companies not to charge enough for their product or service. Most of the time, what lies at the root of this is fear. I've lost count of the times I've urged clients to raise their fees. Whenever they do, they never skip a beat. Dan Sullivan has a great rule of thumb when choosing your pricing. He suggests that you think about the number that scares you and then add 20 percent.

6. Not Staying True to Your Core

Every business has a core focus. Your job is to clearly figure out what yours is as soon as possible. Your business's core is a combination of what you're great at doing and what you're absolutely passionate about. Your job is to make sure that every system, person, and process in your business is designed and aligned to drive that core focus with absolute consistency. And to not get distracted by all the shiny stuff that could inevitably pull you away from your core, diluting focus, and creating chaos and complexity.

7. Not Knowing Your Numbers

One of the most important things you, as an entrepreneur, need to do is make sure you're generating a profit as soon as possible. To do so, you must have a pulse on your numbers. A few simple disciplines for achieving this are for you to (1) review your financials every month; (2) manage a monthly expense budget; and (3) track the five to fifteen most critical numbers for your business every week (e.g., visitors, followers, leads, appointments, proposals, sales, revenue, errors, customer satisfaction, cash balance, accounts payable, accounts receivable). The numbers and data never lie.

8. Not Crystallizing Roles and Responsibilities

To avoid people tripping over each other and creating chaos, each one of your people—including yourself—must know exactly what they're accountable for. That means having a coherent organization chart in place (even if you only have one employee), so that the right hand always knows what the left hand is doing. You must make it abundantly clear to each of your people exactly what you expect of them.

SUMMARY

Now that you've seen the nightmare scenario and the eight critical mistakes, it's important to understand they can be avoided.

This concludes Part II: Glimpse. The objective was to show you what businesses are available to you, share success stories, and show you the dream and nightmare scenarios entrepreneurs live. It's now time to move on to show you the path to taking your leap. But before going on to part III, please take a few minutes to jot down your thoughts from this chapter. What mistakes do you want to avoid? What are your three biggest takeaways or a-has?

WORKSHEET

_____

_____

_____

_____

_____

_____

_____

_____

_____

_____

_____

_____

_____

_____

_____

_____

_____

_____

What actions can you take in the next seven days to make sure you avoid the nightmare scenario?

_____

_____

_____

_____

_____

_____

_____

_____

_____

_____

_____

_____

_____

_____

_____

_____

_____

_____

_____

_____

_____

PART III

PATH

You've made it to the final level. Part III will show you the path to take to increase your odds of entrepreneurial success. I've shared that other careers have paths. So why can't entrepreneurs have a path?

Armed with the right knowledge, you can avoid half the mistakes you might make on your entrepreneurial journey. The other half are inevitable, necessary, and unavoidable. You'll hit a few potholes and change a few tires. Mistakes are part of the learning process. Frankly, you may still fail even if you avoid the mistakes you would have otherwise made. Rather than a failsafe plan, I'm showing you a road that is a little less bumpy than the usual one. You're still going to be jostled by plenty of bumps. You must learn from your mistakes, as they are lessons.

As we embark on the path, I want to prepare you for what's in store. First, we're going to address education—both higher education and the school of hard knocks. From there, we'll look at the benefits of pursuing your passion: how to find your passion and how doing so will increase your odds of success.

We'll then discuss the value of mentorship. A mentor can impart years of experience in a fraction of that time, help you avoid train wrecks, and help get you to where you want to go faster. I'll share the exact steps for finding the mentor who's right for you.

Having achieved clarity on the importance of education, passion, and mentorship, we'll take action and begin your journey, helping you make your entrepreneurial leap and start your business. I'll share the nine stages of building your business, and then offer some helpful resources for a lifetime of growth, learning, and motivation. At the end of each chapter, you'll have an opportunity to capture your thoughts and ideas on a worksheet.

The best way to think about following the entrepreneur's path is passing a series of guideposts. Since everyone is different, the details of every entrepreneur's road to success are unique. But at a high level, every entrepreneur's path has the same stages, which I want to show you to expedite your journey.

To return to an earlier point, being an entrepreneur and starting a successful business are hard. In the process of writing this book, Mike Nehra of Vintage King Audio pleaded with me to make that clear. "It's not just really hard and stressful at times. It also can cause disruption to family, friends, and marriages. It can be an obsessive beast, difficult to tame, and it can hurt your physical well-being. It can keep you awake at night, knowing you're personally tied to the financial ups and downs and responsible for the livelihood of ten, fifty, a hundred-plus people." He goes on to say, "However, many rewards from owning a business include the ability to be creative, the freedom of lifestyle, the positive impact we have on thousands of customers in our space, and it beats working for someone else."

You can think of the path the way you do about your health. If you want to get in peak shape, feel great, and have unlimited energy, a trainer can show you how to work out, when to work out, what to eat, how much to eat, and when to eat. But you then have to make all of the individual decisions and do the work. Only you can decide how to respond to physical and mental setbacks and challenges. Only you can get yourself to work out consistently, push your limits, choose the right foods, and say no to the wrong ones.

Similarly, I can only show the way. You have to make all of the decisions, do the hard work, and be consistently disciplined. With the stage set for part III, let's take the first step on your path.

Chapter 10

College or Not?

Some of the readers of this book are young, pre-college age. If you're at a stage when you're in college or contemplating whether to go to college, this chapter is for you. All other readers can skip this chapter if you choose.

I first want to make it clear that this chapter is not intended to talk you either into or out of going to college. The short answer to the question "College or not?" is that when in doubt, you should probably go to college. With that said, the purpose of this chapter is to create clarity around the reasons an entrepreneur-in-the-making should go to college. Here's the data, and you decide for yourself what's best for you.

For the last twenty years, I've asked every successful entrepreneur who has a college degree the following question: "As an entrepreneur, do you use anything you learned from your degree?" The answer is no almost 100 percent of the time. This includes many MBAs. These answers shocked me initially, until I decided to probe deeper.

THE FOLLOW-UP QUESTIONS

To be completely honest, when I first decided to write this book (based on the answer to the above question), I really thought I was going to be writing a chapter advocating that if you want to be an entrepreneur, you shouldn't go to college. However, since then I've come to a quite different realization. Because, for the last year, I've added two follow-up questions to my first one.

The first follow-up question is: What did you get out of college that helped you become a better entrepreneur?

The second: Would you go back to college if you knew everything you knew today, and if so, what classes would you take?

The responses to these follow-up questions were very telling and, frankly, changed my thinking.

The answers to the first follow-up question mostly described the value of the social benefits, relationships, and connections that entrepreneurs developed in college, which later served them well. Many also said college gave them an opportunity to be entrepreneurial by starting businesses and selling things to fellow students.

As for the second follow-up question, in almost every case, entrepreneurs said they'd definitely go to college again if they had to do it over. However, they said the types of classes they would take would be different.

Here's a list of classes those entrepreneurs would recommend to help you become a better entrepreneur:

- entrepreneurship
- psychology
- economics
- finance and accounting ·
- philosophy
- emotional intelligence
- sales
- negotiation
- leadership
- management
- marketing
- communications
- storytelling
- improvisation/drama
- debate
- public speaking
- technical writing
- computer programming (coding)
- organizational development/behavior
- creative writing
- business law

Based on the answers to the above questions, it probably makes sense for most entrepreneurs-in-the-making to go to college. If you do, however, go in with your eyes wide open, knowing how a college education and the college experience will actually help you as an entrepreneur. Know why you're going and don't just follow the herd.

People are often surprised when they learn I never went to college. I knew very early it wasn't for me. I graduated high school with a solid 2.3 GPA, and I couldn't wait to get out of academia. It was a decision I've never regretted. I simply wanted to get to work and make money. I had very specific income goals for the next ten years and, incidentally, hit them all. While not going to college was my choice, it did make my path harder. Some people looked down on me and made the road tougher.

If you make the same choice, you'll be faced with the same headwinds. In our current society, you're taking a gamble when you decide not to get a degree, as you're limiting your options if you fail as an entrepreneur. I urged both my kids to go to college, which they did. Just like a pro athlete who doesn't develop any other skills, options are limited if you don't make it to the big leagues.

LIFE WITHOUT COLLEGE

While I didn't go to college, I spent many weekends at the colleges my friends attended and received many of the social benefits.

Even though I wanted no more of the formal educational structure, I've always been a fanatic about learning. Every year for the last thirty years, I've typically spent 5 percent of my gross income on education. I've read and listened to hundreds of books, attended hundreds of hours of training, and spent a lot of time learning from peers and mentors. I've spent many hundreds of thousands of dollars on education. While I didn't go to college, I've spent enough time and money to earn a college degree many times over.

I chose to get educated my way, the way I learn best. I have ADHD, OCD, and a touch of dyslexia. I'm a slow learner and a slow reader. I don't memorize well. I would be doomed in a normal college program, just as I was in high school.

If you don't go to college, you must still get educated your way, according to your interests. You can still get an education without college, sometimes a better one. Mark Twain made a remark that fits well here: "I have never let my schooling interfere with my education."

The real world is a great teacher.

Entrepreneurs-in-the-making with the six essential traits learn in a variety of ways. Choose the system that's best for you.

Kazim Ladimeji's Recruiter.com article "5 Surprising Signs You Might Be an Entrepreneur in the Making" lists the five signs as follows:

1. You dropped out of university.
2. You never attended university in the first place.
3. You just don't fit the school system.
4. You hate authority and the way things are.
5. You think your current employer's strategies suck.

In an enlightening Entrepreneur.com blog post, "Richard Branson on Why Entrepreneurs Sometimes Struggle with Formal Education," Branson, founder of the Virgin empire, who dropped out of high school, states:

> *Many students want to know how I was able to start my own career while I was a young student, struggling with my schoolwork, and how I eventually got people to take me seriously as an entrepreneur.*
>
> *Often, their frustration in the classroom was a result of impatience. The greats were eager to get out and build their businesses, which pushed them to drop out of high school or forego college, in order to follow their dreams . . . One thing that entrepreneurs have in common is a talent for seeing things differently. This allows them to identify important gaps in markets, or the need for new sectors to serve specific customer demands.*
>
> *But this ability often leads budding entrepreneurs to rebel against the conformity that is common in traditional education . . . My curiosity often got me into trouble with*

teachers . . . I had dyslexia. When I was a young student, this learning disability was poorly researched and was often mistaken for laziness or a poor ability to learn . . . But my learning disability has never been a setback—it actually gave me a great advantage in business since I have been able to bring a different perspective to problems and challenges, which often enables me to see solutions more clearly.

So in many ways, my education has been my career. For almost 50 years, Virgin's varied collection of businesses and nonprofits means that I have studied and come to understand many sectors. Aviation, banking, media, hospitality, and the fitness industry, to name a few. In the end, solutions to big problems such as these won't come from doing school reports, but by getting out there, asking questions, seeing things differently, and finding the answers ourselves.

In a *Forbes* article titled "Make Way for Generation Z Entrepreneurs Saying No to College," Kaytie Zimmerman writes: "Generation Z have watched millennials rack up hundreds of thousands in student loan debt, all for a four-year degree that has earned them meager entry-level wages. This sobering reality has led many of them to take a serious look at the value of a college degree."

Young entrepreneurs often have the seed planted in them long before they're deciding if they should pursue higher education or start a business. According to a Gallup student poll,

40 percent of students grades five to twelve plan to start their own businesses, while 24 percent are already learning how to start and run a business.

If you choose not to go to college, you're in good company. Here are some other entrepreneurs you might recognize who don't have degrees either:

- Bill Gates, principal founder of Microsoft: dropped out of Harvard
- Evan Williams, cofounder of Twitter: spent a year and a half at the University of Nebraska
- Jan Koum, founder of WhatsApp: dropped out of college
- Richard Branson, founder of the Virgin empire: dropped out of high school
- Russell Simmons, founder of Def Jam: dropped out of college
- Michael Dell, founder of Dell Computers: dropped out of college
- Stacy Ferreira, founder of MySocialCloud: dropped out of college
- Ralph Lauren, founder of the Ralph Lauren Corporation: dropped out of college
- John Mackey, founder of Whole Foods: dropped out of college
- Steve Jobs, cofounder of Apple: dropped out of college

- Dave Thomas, founder of Wendy's: dropped out of high school
- David Green, cofounder of Hobby Lobby with a $7.2 billion net worth: never went to college
- Larry Ellison: cofounder of Oracle Corporation: dropped out of college
- Rachael Ray, celebrity chef and talk show host: dropped out of college
- Anne F. Beiler, founder of Auntie Anne's pretzels: dropped out of high school
- Debbi Fields, creator of Mrs. Fields Original Cookies: attended two years at a community college
- Joyce Hall, founder of Hallmark Cards: never went to college
- Mary Kay Ash, founder of Mary Kay Cosmetics: never went to college
- Ray Kroc, instrumental in the building of McDonald's: dropped out of high school
- Sean John Combs, recording artist and entertainer: dropped out of college
- Walt Disney, cofounder of Disney: dropped out of high school

Along these lines, billionaire Peter Thiel, who cofounded PayPal and is a venture capitalist in Silicon Valley, founded the Thiel Fellowship, an organization that "gives $100,000 to young people who want to build new things instead of sitting in a class-room." His fellowship pays entrepreneurs-in-the-making not to go to college and to get a head start on taking their leap.

Again, don't think that this chapter is biased or anti-college. Most school-age people reading this book should probably go to college. And they will receive tremendous benefits as an entrepreneur-in-the-making.

In fairness, here's a list of successful entrepreneurs who have a college degree. If you choose to go to college, you're also in good company.

- Andrew Mason, founder of Groupon
- Bob Parsons, founder of GoDaddy
- Chad Hurley, cofounder of YouTube
- Craig Newmark, founder of Craigslist
- David Packard, cofounder of Hewlett-Packard
- Fred Smith, founder of FedEx
- Gordon Moore, cofounder of Intel
- Herb Kelleher, cofounder of Southwest Airlines
- Jeff Bezos, founder of Amazon
- Jerry Yang, cofounder of Yahoo!
- John Schnatter, founder of Papa John's
- John W. Marriott, founder of Marriott Corporation
- Larry Page, cofounder of Google
- Mark Cuban, cofounder of Broadcast.com

- Martha Stewart, founder of Martha Stewart Living Omnimedia
- Oprah Winfrey, founder of Harpo Inc.
- Phil Knight, cofounder of Nike
- Pierre Omidyar, founder of eBay
- Ralph J. Roberts, cofounder of Comcast Communications
- Reed Hastings, cofounder of Netflix
- Sam Walton, founder of Walmart
- Sergey Brin, cofounder of Google
- Vera Wang, founder of Vera Wang

One last statistic that you might find interesting is a 2017 CNBC/Survey Monkey Small Business Survey. It showed that most small-business owners in the United States don't have a college degree, while 44 percent of small-business owners have a four-year degree or higher.

SUMMARY

You must decide the right educational path for you, as an entrepreneur-in-the-making. Remember: when in doubt, you're probably better off going to college.

Before we move on, please take a few minutes and jot down your thoughts on this chapter. What's the right path for you?

What action can you take in the next seven days to help you make the best decision regarding the right path for you?

WORKSHEET

_____

_____

_____

_____

_____

_____

_____

_____

_____

_____

_____

_____

_____

_____

_____

_____

_____

_____

_____

_____

_____

_____

_____

_____

_____

_____

What action can you take in the next seven days to help you make the best decision regarding the right path for you?

_____

_____

_____

_____

_____

_____

_____

_____

_____

You can download all worksheets and tools at

e-leap.com.

CHAPTER 11

DISCOVER YOUR PASSION

This chapter starts by offering you two options. Option one: you spend the next ten years of your life working on something you couldn't care less about. Option two: you spend the next ten years working on something you're passionate about.

Which option seems better to you?

Option two is the obvious choice. That's why we'll focus on the following:

1. Helping you discover what your passion is
2. Convincing you that it's possible to build a business around your passion
3. Giving you examples of how people have done it

THE POWER OF PASSION

Building a business around something you have a deep passion for will be one of the main reasons you'll succeed. It's what will get you through the tough times, past the roadblocks, and over the barriers. Passion gives you superhuman strength and unlimited energy.

Here's what Steve Jobs, cofounder of Apple, says about passion in an emotionally impactful YouTube video:

> *People say you have to have a lot of passion for what you are doing, and it's totally true. The reason is because [business] is so hard that if you don't, any rational person would give up. It's really hard, and you have to do it over a sustained period of time, so if you don't love it and you are not having fun doing it, you're going to give up. That's what happens to most people, actually. If you really look at the ones that ended up being successful, in the eyes of society, and the ones that didn't, oftentimes the ones that are successful loved what they did. They could persevere when it got really tough, and the ones that didn't love it quit, because they are sane. Who would want to put up with this stuff if you don't love it? It's a lot of hard work, and it's a lot of worrying constantly, and if you don't love it, you're going to fail. [youtu.be/PznJqxon4zE]*

Peter Diamandis, author of *Abundance: The Future Is Better Than You Think*, when asked what advice he wishes he had been given when he was starting out, said:

> *Be clear about your passion and don't settle for anything else. Don't do something for the money, or to make your parents or your teachers happy. Pursue a start-up business because it's your personal passion, your highest aspiration. If you do something you are passionate about, you will work harder than ever before and outshine anyone. Doing anything big and bold is difficult, and if you're not totally in love with what you're doing, you'll give up before you succeed.*

If you research the source of the word *passion*, you'll learn that the Latin root is "suffering." Passionate people suffer for their cause. A passion, purpose, or cause typically stems from a wound, tough experience, void, or need. The reason I love helping entrepreneurs run better businesses is because I was thrown into the fire of saving my dad's business. The reason I'm writing this book is because once I was an entrepreneur-in-the-making and felt lost.

In his article "A Single Individual Driven by a Purpose Can Change the World," Diamandis also writes:

> *I often get asked for a single piece of advice to make an entrepreneur succeed. While there is no surefire route to*

success, I believe a necessary component of success for every entrepreneur is having a Massively Transformative Purpose (MTP). A purpose that drives you to wake up in the morning. Something you repeat in your head while you eat, shower, and before you go to sleep. Every successful person and organization has an MTP. An MTP must be something that inspires and challenges you. It must be aimed not just at the mind, but also the heart. It has to be declared with confidence and sincerity. It can't be a narrow goal, or even technology specific. And above all, it has to be uniquely yours.

THE SEARCH FOR YOUR PASSION

Now let's talk about how to find *your* passion. There have been many variations of this concept. Over time, passion has also been described as your purpose, cause, calling, your why, your obsession or mission.

Right now, *passion* is a popular term for this topic. In its simplest form, you're figuring out the dent you want to put in the universe—be it a huge dent or a little one. It's irrelevant what word you use, as long as it gets your blood pumping. In the words of my friend Burke Miller, the author of *A Sacred Trust: The Four Disciplines of Conscious Leadership*, "Your purpose is a confluence of what you are built for, and what you stand for."

Another way of saying it is that you've got to figure out your reason for being, why you exist. You might already know it, which would be great, but if not, that's okay. You have plenty of time. What follows will hopefully give you a light bulb moment.

It's important that you don't let anyone discourage you. Your passion is going to come from you and only you. If you share your calling with someone who is not impressed, ignore their reaction. Your passion is not going to excite everyone. The passion of one client of mine was light bulbs, of all things, and he built his company into one of the largest light bulb distributors in the country.

Mary Kay built an empire to "provide women with unlimited opportunity." Walt Disney wanted "to make people happy." EOS Worldwide's purpose is "to help entrepreneurs live their ideal lives." Nike's is "to bring inspiration and innovation to every athlete in the world."

Some questions to help you find your passion might be: What did you love to do when you were a kid, teen, or young adult? What do you love to do now? On what topics do your friends ask your advice? What gives you energy while thinking about it or doing it? What are your hobbies? Which of your talents or skills are you most proud of?

While helping many people discover what drives them, I've found their passions tend to fall into one of four broad categories:

1. Helping and serving the customer or client
2. Building an amazing company

3. Solving problems and innovating

4. Winning: being the best or the biggest

See which of those four broad categories you're drawn to. Not so much the words, but the category. This will help you narrow the field. You'll then use your own words to help make that passion your own.

Another helpful tool to help you create clarity around finding your passion is Dr. Gary Sanchez's "9 WHYS." Gary is the author of *Move Forward Faster* and believes your passion comes from knowing your WHY, HOW, and WHAT. He says that when WHAT you do is in line with WHY you do it and HOW you want to express it, you'll have passion for what you do. And passion is the fuel that gives you the energy to pursue your dreams.

Focusing on the WHY part of the equation, here are Gary's 9 WHYS. He believes all people have one of them. To discover your WHY, go to whyinstitute.com and use the free WHY app, which takes about four minutes. Here are the 9 WHYS.

1. To **Contribute** to a greater cause, to add value
2. To create relationships based on **Trust**
3. To **Make Sense** out of complex things
4. To find a **Better Way** and share it
5. To do things the **Right Way**
6. To **Challenge** the status quo with new thinking
7. To seek **Mastery** and understanding

8. To create **Clarity**

9. To **Simplify**

Keep in mind that you should use these suggestions as guides. There's no one answer that fits every entrepreneur.

Next, try a great thought exercise that might also help you identify your passion. It takes about thirty minutes and has three steps.

Step 1. List your top three successes.

Step 2. List your top three failures.

Step 3. Based on the answers to the above questions, what has life prepared you for?

The answer in the third step might shed some light on finding your calling. It helped me a great deal.

SUMMARY

As Steve Jobs put it, "The only way to be truly satisfied is to do what you believe is great work. And the only way to do great work is to love what you do. If you haven't found it yet, keep looking. Don't settle. As with all matters of the heart, you'll know when you find it."

That brings you a little closer, I hope, to finding your passion. Please take a few minutes to write your insights and list any passions you can think of. Also, consider doing the thirty-minute exercise.

WORKSHEET

_____

_____

_____

_____

_____

_____

_____

_____

_____

_____

_____

_____

_____

_____

_____

_____

_____

The Thirty-Minute
Three-Step Exercise

Step 1. List your top three successes:

_____

_____

_____

_____

_____

_____

_____

_____

_____

Step 2. List your top three failures:

_____

_____

_____

_____

_____

_____

_____

_____

_____

_____

Step 3. Based on the answers to the above questions, what has life prepared you for?

_____

_____

_____

_____

_____

_____

_____

_____

What action can you take in the next seven days to discover your passion?

_____

_____

_____

_____

_____

_____

_____

_____

_____

_____

You can download all worksheets and tools at

e-leap.com.

CHAPTER 12

FIND A MENTOR

A mentor is an experienced and trusted advisor, counselor, or guide. Mentorship involves finding someone who is where you want to be and asking that person to take you under their wing and teach you everything they know.

If you want to be a successful entrepreneur and build a $10 million software-development company, imagine how you would increase your odds of success and speed up your path if the founder of a $10 million software-development company was willing to become a trusted guide. They know about all the mistakes you're about to make, and they can help you dodge them, shaving years off your learning curve.

Having a mentor is like having a speed pass. Back when I played video games with my kids, Mario Kart was very popular, and it featured a speed strip on the racetrack. If you were skillful enough to drive over it, your car would zoom past the others. Having a mentor is like having an entrepreneurial speed strip.

APPRENTICESHIP: AN OVERLOOKED, UNDERVALUED STEP ON THE PATH

For thousands of years, masters of their craft would take apprentices under their wing and teach them everything they knew. Protégés would learn at the feet of their masters and, when ready, go out on their own. Many apprentices became better and more successful than their masters.

Today you can find apprenticeship programs for plumbers, carpenters, masons, and steelworkers. Why not for entrepreneurs? While there isn't a formal entrepreneurial apprenticeship program (yet), you can create your own—simply by finding a mentor.

As I mentioned earlier, I had two mentors in my twenties: my dad, Floyd Wickman, and Sam Cupp. My mentoring relationship with my dad, which changed my life, was very informal. My relationship with Sam Cupp was much more structured. I met with Sam for an hour and a half every other month for four years. I would share all my ideas and issues, and he would impart his wisdom and perspectives. I remember feeling so excited and nervous going to those meetings at his office. He continued to mentor me less formally for another ten years, until his sudden passing in his early sixties while playing ice hockey, one of his passions. I miss him greatly. He put a huge dent in the universe.

Although having a mentor has many advantages and benefits, you should realize that you can still become successful without a mentor. In my interviews with successful entrepreneurs, I discovered that more than half had mentors when they were starting out. Those that didn't still found success. However, speaking from experience, I believe success will be more likely with a mentor.

Don't be discouraged if you can't find a mentor right now. Sometimes you have to do some looking around for the right person. Also, finding a mentor at this time might not feel right to you, and that's okay too.

FINDING A MENTOR

So how do you find a mentor? My dad was a mentor not only to me but also to many others, including Terri Sjodin, a very successful entrepreneur and speaker. In 1996, my father and Terri wrote the proverbial "book on mentoring" entitled *Mentoring: The Most Obvious Yet Overlooked Key to Achieving More in Life Than You Ever Dreamed Possible,* which, unfortunately, is out of print. It was an incredibly helpful and fascinating book because it's written from both a mentor and a protégé's points of view, laying out a step-by-step process for finding and managing a mentor relationship.

Here's a high-level overview of the process they recommend.

First, think about what you want to build as an entrepreneur. Then determine the type of person who is where you want to be. This potential mentor doesn't always have to be an entrepreneur in exactly the same business. You have to consider that competition might be an issue in such cases, and a potential mentor who would be a direct competitor might resist the idea of teaching you trade secrets. You might find someone who's in the same industry with a different size business.

You may already know who you want as a mentor. It might be someone you admire. Please make sure you have multiple candidates because you may hear some nos. These are very busy people. Their refusal is not a reflection of you. Once you've identified your candidates, the second step is to reach out and schedule the first meeting. In that meeting, share your story, ask them to share their story, and passionately ask for what you want from them—to mentor you.

Again, you may hear some nos. Once you get a yes, the next step is to agree on a format. Again, Sam and I met every other month for ninety minutes, and I would bring my questions, ideas, and issues.

CULTIVATING YOUR MENTOR RELATIONSHIP

My dad and Terri offered two additional insights. First, over the course of the relationship, it's critical that you show your mentor you're applying what you're learning from them. A great mentor who passes along their knowledge wants to know it's being put to work.

My dad is a hall-of-fame motivational speaker in the National Speakers Association. His mentor was Zig Ziglar, the greatest motivational speaker of all time. Zig was very much in demand, and my dad didn't understand why Zig would always make time to take his calls. One day he asked Zig straight out why he took his calls. Zig responded, "Floyd, it's because I hear *of* you and *from* you. You always follow up and let me know how things went." This was Zig's way of saying that my dad was applying the advice Zig was giving him.

The second important insight is to constantly express gratitude for your mentor's time. Show you appreciate your mentor's valuable commitment. Say thank you, often.

STAGES OF MENTORING

You should realize also that the mentor you find at this stage of your entrepreneurial career might be different from the one you need in the next stage. You might first find a mentor who just took their entrepreneurial leap and is able to mentor you in doing that. Then you might find a mentor who helps your business grow to ten employees, and then another who helps it get to a thousand.

Mentoring has many variables. Some relationships are short, lasting only a year. You may also have multiple mentors. One entrepreneur I interviewed had ten mentors over twenty years. By contrast, other relationships will last a lifetime.

One last note on mentoring. You should also consider going to work for an entrepreneur who's where you want to be. Imagine being able to spend every day inside their business. If the opportunity to learn is advantageous enough, and they're not willing or able to pay you, you might work for free or at least for less than market compensation. This is like going to school but not having to pay tuition.

At the least, shadow an entrepreneur for a day, week, or month, so you can see what the real world of entrepreneurship looks like. Watching your mentor deal with financial, customer, and employee issues, cash crunches, and back-to-back meetings is invaluable.

SUMMARY

Up until this point, we've been laying a foundation: clarifying the role of college in your journey, discovering your passion, and exploring the value of mentoring. We now shift to action, taking your leap and building your business. Before we do, please take a few minutes and jot down your insights on mentoring. Think about the type of mentor you want and who might make a great mentor. Maybe it's someone you already know—a parent, aunt, uncle, or friend of the family. Maybe it's someone you admire but have never met. Write down your thoughts, ideas, fears, and concerns.

WORKSHEET

_____

_____

_____

_____

_____

_____

_____

_____

_____

_____

_____

_____

_____

_____

_____

_____

_____

What action can you take in the next seven days to find a mentor?

_____

_____

_____

_____

_____

_____

_____

_____

_____

_____

_____

_____

_____

You can download all worksheets and tools at

e-leap.com.

CHAPTER 13

TAKE ACTION AND BE PATIENT

N ow that you know you're an entrepreneur-in-the-making, it's time to take action. At the same time, you must also be patient. This might feel like a contradiction in terms. "Take action" makes you feel like you need to put the pedal to the metal. "Be patient" makes you feel like you need to slam on the brakes. So, what gives?

While these two instructions may sound contradictory, they're actually quite complementary. By doing both you can manage your expectations and avoid a lot of frustration. If you think that you're going to finish this book today, have your idea tomorrow, launch your business next week, and generate $5 million next year—well, most of you are going to be disappointed. That's why you need to both "take action" and "be patient."

TEN-YEAR THINKING—THE
VIRTUE OF PATIENCE

You can afford to be patient because you know you're going to make your mark someday. It might be next week or fifteen years from now. As you patiently move toward your goal, you have to reframe your sense of time. Try to think in ten-year time frames. Regardless of your age, your jaw may have just dropped. Those of you aged eleven to nineteen who are reading this have, after all, only lived one full ten-year time frame. But there's a good reason for this.

I learned the discipline of thinking in ten-year time frames when I was thirty-five. Once I did, time slowed down. I started having more fun. I was less frustrated and rushed, and more great things started happening.

The process works like this. First, you have to understand that, barring a natural disaster or getting run over by a car, you're probably going to live until age eighty-five. Even if you're sixty-five right now, you still have a good twenty years left. If you're fifteen, you have seventy years left.

Next, you need to realize that you can accomplish anything in ten years, worst case twenty. As in the old business axiom, "It takes twenty years to become an overnight success."

If you think you'll build an empire in the next couple of years, in most cases you're going to be sorely disappointed. If you accept that you have ten years to build something great, your mind and your body can relax. You'll think better and make better decisions.

You might be a fifty-one-year-old stay-at-home mom who is now an empty-nester trying to find herself. You say to yourself, "I know I'm an entrepreneur-in-the-making, and someday I'm going to take my leap." You've put your intention out there to the universe. Next year, after trying a few things, you discover your passion and start a business around it. At age sixty, you're making more money than you could have ever imagined, having more fun, and feeling more fulfilled than ever.

Or if you're seventeen years old and reading this, you might say to yourself, "I'm an entrepreneur-in-the-making. I know I'm going to be an entrepreneur someday. I'm going to go to college and take the right classes. Then I'll get a few different jobs until I find my calling." You might take your leap when you're twenty-six, and at thirty-five, you're making a million dollars (or $100,000, whatever's important to you), running a business you love, and making a huge impact on the world.

You can accomplish anything in ten years, but rarely in two. The motivational speaker Les Brown used to say, "All you need is a good decade." Part of the reason is that this current phase is usually filled with false starts. Whatever you do between now and when you open for business is all part of the process. It will often seem to have no direct correlation to the business you finally start. But it does. As Rosabeth Moss Kanter says, "In the middle, everything looks like failure."

I took my leap at age twenty-five. Between the ages of eighteen and twenty-four, I worked in a machine shop, sold corporate travel, had a mail-order company, and invested in and sold real estate. None of this had a direct correlation with a training company, but I can recall dozens of experiences from those different endeavors that are now all part of what I know as an entrepreneur.

The idea is to move forward. Try a lot of things. Learn lessons. Just do something. Get to work, get a job, work harder than everyone, and the inspiration will come. This is your experimental testing phase. It's as much about figuring out what you don't like as it is figuring out what you love. In the back of your mind, you know what and who you are. You have put what you're going to be out there into the universe, and, assuming you're committed to becoming an entrepreneur, the answers will come.

Of course, there may be the reader of this book who's eighteen, just graduated high school, and quickly finds their passion. They decide not to go to college and start a business at nineteen that generates millions in revenue. And they may become a billionaire by age twenty-five.

That scenario is the exception. Truly, one in a million. If you measure yourself against them, you'll always feel like a failure. Ironically, if you're patient and think in ten-year time frames, you'll probably get to where you want to go faster.

As you embark on this somewhat messy next phase, your job is to keep your eyes peeled for your inspiration. Think about a need you see or problem to be solved. As marketing guru Joe Polish says, "Most of the money we make in the world comes from transforming other people's bad news into good news." And Richard Rossi says, "Wherever there is anxiety, there is opportunity."

Dan Sullivan says, "When people are feeling confused, isolated and powerless, there is an opportunity."

Here's a list of entrepreneurial "light bulb moments" that were turned into businesses. Here's hoping they give you such a moment:

- a software program that helps landscapers run their businesses better
- a wedge to stop food from falling in between your car seats
- a sales training program for real estate agents
- a protein bar made from crickets
- remanufacturing toner cartridges for printers
- buying defective iPod minis, fixing and reselling them
- an app that helps people meditate
- portable photo booths for events
- buying used audio equipment low and reselling it high
- a foldable kayak
- a ring for your finger that monitors your sleep, steps, and other vitals
- organizing people's homes

- eye-catching basketball socks
- cleaning cars, boats, jets
- direct-to-consumer braces for your teeth
- shared electronic scooters in cities
- a video camera for your front door
- selling ugly Christmas sweaters
- food trucks
- mobile windshield crack repair
- a more interactive golf range
- an app that gives you leadership insight
- a warehouse full of trampolines to entertain kids
- opening a salad place in a college town
- starting a fantasy sports advisory service
- compact fitness equipment
- a software platform that helps people share a ride, a room, a couch
- a tracking device to help you find your keys
- a salsa company
- buying and selling items on Amazon, eBay, and Alibaba
- a mobile platform to help entertainers monetize their brands and fans

To get your gears turning a little bit more, here's a short list of possible businesses:

Appliance Repair	Home Building
Beauty Salon	Home Inspection
Bicycle Repair	Home Maintenance
Boat Cleaning	Household Organizing
Candy Making	Interior Decorator
Carpentry	Import-Export Specialist
Child Care Services	Jewelry Making
Cleaning Service	Limousine Service
Clothing Manufacturer	Micro-Brewing
Computer Repair	Moving Company
Editorial Services	Nutrition Counseling
Electronics Repair	Personal Concierge
Event Planning	Personal Trainer
Fence Installation	Physical Therapy
Financial Planner	Property Management
Furniture Making	Spa Services
Gift Basket Service	Tattoo Removal
Graffiti Removal	Wedding Planner

Peter Diamandis offers this advice for entrepreneurs-in-the-making who are trying to find their start-up idea: "Historically, I come up with my best ideas when reading a book."

I've come up with my best ideas both from books and when brainstorming with friends and colleagues I respect, who bring different perspectives or areas of expertise to the table. Diamandis also adds this advice:

Throughout my career, whenever I've started a company just to make money, it's been a mistake. Starting any successful company is always hard work, and if my heart isn't in it, the effort becomes hard, unfulfilling work, and I give up before the job is done.

On the flip side, when I start a company to solve a problem truly important to me, one that excites me, even if the solution takes ten years, every one of those ten years are well spent, educational, and fulfilling.

ENTREPRENEURS WHO TOOK THEIR LEAP

Here are a handful of stories about entrepreneurs-in-the-making who took their leap and how they got their inspiration.

Watching my friend Ed Pobur's son grow up, I knew he was an entrepreneur-in-the-making. The six essential traits are actually quite obvious in people when you're aware of them. In eighth grade, Eddie Pobur Jr. started a lawn-cutting business with his friend. They ran that business until graduating high school. At their peak, they were cutting thirty lawns a week.

When he was sixteen, he started a window-tinting business that made him much more money than lawn cutting. He continued that business until something better came along at age twenty-two.

He grew up in a golf course community. All his life he was surrounded by golf carts. His sophomore year in college, he started a golf cart sales and service business, Eddie's Golf Carts. In his first year, he sold thirty golf carts; in his second year, he sold eighty golf carts; and in his fifth year, he will sell and service over two hundred golf carts. His growth potential is unlimited.

Eddie capitalized on a very hot trend, the market for customized golf carts, which continues to grow rapidly.

Shelly Sun, the founder of BrightStar Care, was a thirty-one-year old corporate controller in the airline industry when she had her light bulb moment.

She was faced with a common family issue. She had to find in-home health care for her family member, who had stage four cancer. It required all levels of care and was a challenging and exhausting experience. She realized a huge gap in the industry's ability to provide a full continuum of care for her loved one.

She saw an opportunity to improve the industry and help many families avoid the frustrations and heartaches she experienced.

Around the same time, she read the book *Rich Dad, Poor Dad* by Robert Kiyosaki. The book helped her realize that it might be just as risky to stay in corporate America as it is to become an entrepreneur.

So she gave herself a year to make it work. She did exhaustive research, talking to hospitals, caregivers, and nursing homes. Her goal was to create a complete in-home solution for families who need to care for a sick loved one, and give them peace of mind.

Shelly launched her first location in Illinois and then opened two more over the next two years. By year three, she decided to franchise her concept. She sold her second and third locations to franchisees in order to fund the franchising model. The business took off from there. Sixteen years later, Shelly now has 335 locations, and BrightStar Care generates $440 million in system-wide sales.

Scott Bade of ImageSoft is a classic example of someone who waited for their inspiration. He was living his passion, working as a computer programmer and salesperson for a software company for nine years, until he decided it was time at age thirty-seven. He took his leap in 1999 to start his own software company. Shortly after, he joined forces with two other partners, James Leneschmidt and Steve Glisky. He and his partners have since built ImageSoft into a $28 million company with 130 employees.

Dan Haynes was a sophomore in high school when he had his light bulb moment and took his entrepreneurial leap. One of his passions is online gaming. Yet he was getting tired of the same old characters. So he decided to create his own game.

At first, it was just for fun. He wasn't thinking of it as a business. He was just charging people to use it to cover the cost of hosting servers and the website. But eventually, it took off, and five years later, Dan's video gaming company, Gaminglight, is generating $10,000 a month in profit.

Ryan Findling has always had entrepreneurial wiring. At the tender age of four, he had a successful lemonade stand that he then tried to franchise and sell to his friends. That fledgling attempt failed.

In sixth grade, he started a company called fotofoto, which does photo booths for weddings, bar mitzvahs, and parties. Ryan started the business with a partner, but realized after two weeks, having a partner was not for him. Over the last five years, he has built it up to where he will do two hundred events this year in his junior year of high school and is now planning to sell the business before he graduates high school.

Ryan also just started a new company called Non-Profit Promos. It's a for-profit business that sells promotional products and spirit wear to nonprofits for their fund-raising efforts. He created a very simple online interface for users to order. The site has been up for fifteen days, and he already has fifteen orders.

An *Entrepreneur* magazine edition on young millionaires featured Rachel Zietz, the entrepreneur who founded Gladiator Lacrosse. At thirteen, she started her company to make durable, affordable practice equipment for the sport of lacrosse. Five years later, she is projecting to do $2 million in revenue while attending Princeton as a freshman.

That same *Entrepreneur* edition featured Brennan Agranoff, the founder of HoopSwagg. At age thirteen, he wanted basketball socks that stood out, and he could only find boring or very expensive socks. He saw a need, and after nine months of research and a $3,000 investment from his parents, he was in business. HoopSwagg is described as a playful brand that manufacturers eye-catching athletic socks. After five years, Brennan has twenty employees and is on track to hit $1.6 million in revenue. He's putting off college to focus on building the business.

Marc Schechter, co-owner of Schechter Wealth, a wealth advisory firm, exhibited all the signs of an entrepreneur-in-the-making before taking his leap. At age twelve, he was a DJ and magician at kids' parties; at age sixteen, he became a videographer at parties; and at the age of nineteen when in college, he took his leap with a partner and started Star Trax, which managed karaoke for bars. Having purchased music mixing systems and song lyrics, he was able to create the karaoke concept before karaoke became popular.

Marc initially got into the business with a partner with the idea of doing this karaoke concept at private parties. After seeing how much fun groups of people had doing this at private parties, he decided to expand their services to a local bar one night a week. Marc received 20 percent of the growth in revenues from the bar owner, and his innovation vaulted the bar's sales from a quiet $500 per night to lines out the door and $2,500 per night. Marc himself was making $400 per night. Even more exciting to him than the significant earnings was the recognition and association of being involved with something creative, unique, and valuable.

A year later, Marc had crews working at ten different bars per week. After graduating college, he dropped his plans for Wall

Street in favor of continuing with Star Trax. He bought out his initial partner and sold 50 percent to new partners. Together, they built Star Trax into a very successful multimillion-dollar event-planning company.

At age thirty-five, Marc left Star Trax and sold his share of the business to his partner over subsequent years. Marc then focused his entrepreneurial passion and mind-set on growing his family business, Schechter Wealth. Since he joined the company, it has quintupled in size.

The final story is one that is too good not to add, although I can't find the original source or the entrepreneur's name. If you know who this is, please let me know. The story is that of a young man who, after he got a DUI, was kicked out of his parents' house. Homeless, he slept on the couch of a friend on the Florida coast for a little while. Because he was living near the water, at the end of each day he noticed people gathering around the docks. Curious, he decided to go see what all the fuss was about. He learned that these people were gathering to help clean the fishing boats coming in after a day of fishing.

When he heard what the people were being paid, he had a light bulb moment. He organized a crew and started a boat-cleaning business. In his first year, he made $60,000. Becoming more advanced, he learned how to clean under the boats' hulls, which no one at the docks had previously been able to do. He began cleaning larger boats and then yachts and started a delivery service, taking boats to Mexico for owners who wanted to fly down and sail. His boat-servicing business is now a multimillion-dollar business.

SUMMARY

Once you commit to the fact that you're an entrepreneur-in-the-making, you should think in ten-year time frames, and move forward when you find your calling. Consider reviewing the list of industries in chapter 8 again, as you may now see them in a different light, and the list may prompt additional ideas.

You might need to keep rereading this book before your light bulb moment comes. I believe you'll have new and different insights each read through.

Before we move on to taking your leap, please take a few minutes to jot down the thoughts and ideas this chapter has prompted. You should also write the words "I am an entrepreneur-in-the-making" if you believe it. It also wouldn't hurt to say those words out loud right now.

WORKSHEET

What action can you take in the next seven days to help you have your light bulb moment?

_____

_____

_____

_____

_____

_____

_____

_____

_____

_____

_____

_____

_____

_____

_____

_____

_____

_____

You can download all worksheets and tools at
e-leap.com.

CHAPTER 14

TAKING THE LEAP: STARTING YOUR BUSINESS

You've finally reached the point of taking your leap. As discussed in the previous chapter, the time frame between when you confirm that you're an entrepreneur-in-the-making and when you discover the business you want to start will vary. For some, the process takes days. For others, years. Again, it's never too late to take your leap. Your age is irrelevant.

I should point out that this chapter is not going to address such issues as filing your company as an S corp, C corp, limited partnership, and so on. I won't be teaching you how to open a bank account or design business cards. Frankly, these steps are easy to do, and you'll find many resources readily available to help you. An internet search or calling a local attorney will provide you with the legal and administrative details of starting your company.

I would, however, highly recommend you read Steve

Mariotti's book *The Young Entrepreneur's Guide to Starting and Running a Business.* It's a great resource and how-to manual for you at this stage. It goes into detail about the practical and detailed steps of starting and running a business, along with many inspiring real-life stories.

This chapter is not going to teach how to raise money, either. According to smallbiztrends.com, 86 percent of start-ups don't start with outside capital, and 77 percent of founders rely entirely on personal resources for initial funding. These statistics are consistent with my interviews with successful entrepreneurs. A full 90 percent didn't start with outside funds, and neither did I.

If you're looking to raise outside funds, an internet search will reveal the many resources available, including crowdsourcing, banks, venture capitalists, angel investors, small business loans, and grants. I caution you to be careful and seek expert advice, as some funding sources will take advantage of you. Consider asking your network for funding sources as well. If you intend to raise outside funds, you probably will need a thorough and detailed business plan. If you aren't, you won't. Again, searching the internet will turn up hundreds of business-plan templates. However, 90 percent of the entrepreneurs I've interviewed didn't have a detailed business plan when they started their businesses.

Instead, we're going to focus on key disciplines that will make the difference between succeeding or failing once you take your entrepreneurial leap.

EIGHT DISCIPLINES TO INCREASE YOUR ODDS OF SUCCESS

Assuming you have an idea that you believe has value and are ready to bring it to the world, adopting these eight specific disciplines will increase your odds of succeeding.

Discipline #1: Clarify Your Vision

The first step when taking your leap is to capture your vision in writing. While it's highly unlikely you'll need a detailed business plan (because you won't be raising money), you must have a clear vision in writing.

Documenting your vision is a matter of answering a handful of vital questions. Here are eight questions you'll need to answer in order to clarify your vision.

1. What am I passionate about? (Why am I doing this?)
2. What want or need am I filling for my customer/client?
3. Who is my ideal customer? (Describe your ideal customer.)
4. What's the pricing structure for my product or service?
5. What's the number one most important goal to accomplish in ten years?
6. What will the business look like in three years? (Include your top-line revenue, your personal income, your

profit, and ten bullet points describing exactly what your business will look like in three years.)

7. What do I have to accomplish in the first year? (Include your top-line revenue, your personal income, your profit, and your three to seven most important goals.)

8. What are the three to seven most important things I must accomplish in the next ninety days?

You can download MyVision Clarifier, which is a tool that you can edit at will to capture your vision, at e-leap.com.

By answering these questions, you'll create clarity for yourself and others. Imagine you're going to start a unique jewelry-making business, and you want to generate $2 million in revenue in ten years. Here's what your vision might look like:

1. **What am I passionate about? (Why am I doing this?**
   Helping women make a statement.

2. **What want or need am I filling for my customer/ client?**
   The need for women to express themselves, look great, and be unique.

3. **Who is my ideal customer? (Describe your ideal customer.)**
   Women who are fashion forward and want to be unique, make fashion statements, stand out, and can afford it.

4. **What's the pricing structure for my product or service?**

    I charge a premium for my jewelry: $500 for rings and earrings, $1,000 for bracelets, and $2,000 for necklaces.

5. **What's the number one most important goal to accomplish in ten years?**

    To generate $2 million in revenue and $1 million in profit in 20XX.

6. **What will the business look like in three years? (Include your top-line revenue, your personal income, your profit, and ten bullet points describing exactly what your business will look like in three years.)**

    <u>December 31, 20XX</u>

    $500,000 in revenue

    $125,000 in personal income

    $100,000 in profit

    - sell 500 pieces of jewelry
    - have three employees
    - invest heavily in marketing and in branding
    - have a production facility
    - have a website selling 300 pieces of jewelry
    - have 10 boutique stores selling our jewelry
    - $150,000 in cash reserves
    - have at least one celebrity wearing our jewelry

- hire a PR agency
- featured in at least one prominent media source

7. What do I have to accomplish in the first year? (Include your top-line revenue, your personal income, your profit, and your three to seven most important goals.)

<u>December 31, 20XX</u>
$75,000 in revenue
$30,000 in personal income
$0 in profit

1. Sell 75 pieces of jewelry
2. Launch website
3. Strong social-media presence: 25,000 followers
4. One boutique store selling our jewelry.

8. What are the three to seven most important things I must get done in the next 90 days?

1. Make 10 of each product
2. Sell one of each
3. Get feedback from 20 potential customers

Once you answer these questions, the vision for starting, in this case, your unique jewelry business becomes very clear and will help you stay focused as you're taking your leap. It will also create clarity for any other people involved in the business, such as employees, vendors, partners, and clients, increasing the odds of success. Simply put, the clearer your vision, the more likely you are to succeed.

Discipline #2: Decide if You're a "Partner Person"

Some entrepreneurs desire partners, and some don't. Either will work. I work with both successful entrepreneurs who have one or more partners and other successful entrepreneurs who own 100 percent of their companies and would never have a partner. You just have to decide which type you are.

You might want to own 100 percent and have all the responsibility, with great, well-compensated employees around you. You might want to own a majority of the business and have minority partners who have "skin in the game" and share the responsibility and rewards with you.

On the other hand, you might be more comfortable with an even fifty-fifty partnership or team with two other partners, each of you owning a third. You might want many partners because you prefer to have people "all in" with you, sharing the risk. There are pros and cons to each scenario.

I share this partnership choice up front because I've seen so many horror stories of entrepreneurs who made the wrong choice when taking their leap. Some should have had a partner, because they just shouldn't have gone it alone, and some never should have had partners because they wanted to be in complete control.

Darren Findling, founder of the Probate Pro, PLC, states, "I started building a business with family member partners, and that never should have happened. I was never designed or born to have partners. I was born to lead and collaborate with other leaders, but not to stand shoulder to shoulder in a partnership."

I myself like having a partner, although I need to have controlling interest in the business and be the final decision maker. That's what works best for me. Any scenario can work. Whatever you decide, don't be swayed by what works well for other entrepreneurs. You have to figure out what works best for you.

Partnerships are hard. If you do take your leap with a partner or partners, make sure you're thinking ten years out. Also make sure you want to spend a lot of time with these people and their families, because you'll spend more time with your partners than anyone else in your life. A partnership is truly a business marriage, and you have to make sure you and your partner's core values are completely aligned. From there, consider getting an attorney and a partnership agreement.

Of my 134 clients, 54 have been partnerships. Of those, 22

had serious issues. More than half worked through their issues, but nine parted ways.

Discipline #3: Know That the Bigger the Problem You Solve in the World, the More Successful You'll Be

This discipline is a reminder to constantly stay focused on providing value to your customers or clients. That's because the more value you provide, the more you're worth. The more problems you solve for them and the easier you make their lives, the more money you'll make.

You do this by getting to know your customers and clients better than they know themselves. As Steve Jobs said, "Get closer than ever to your customers. So close that you tell them what they need, well before they realize it themselves."

Far too often, entrepreneurs who begin to achieve some level of success start to get cocky and take the customer for granted. As a result, the original value of the product or service decreases. The lack of attention and innovation allows the competition to catch up, and you begin to lose your customers fast and potentially fail.

Discipline #4: Get Feedback from Customers and Clients Early and Often

The biggest mistake many entrepreneurs make when taking their leap is to assume their customer is going to love their idea. Based on this assumption, they create detailed long-term plans or spend money on the product or marketing before testing it and getting feedback. By contrast, I made sure this book was read by fifty people before it was published. I wanted to know if my target market loved it before I made a big investment.

What I urge you to do instead is work on a simplified premise. Focus first on providing value, then get feedback quickly and often from the people who will be paying you for the product or service. Don't ask your brother, friend, parent, or significant other for feedback. They aren't the ones paying you money. If the people who put down hard cash aren't raving fans, you have nothing, and you have to make a course correction.

When my partner Don and I were eighteen months into launching our business, EOS Worldwide, we had a great product, demand, and a small team of implementers, but we weren't making any money. Our business model wasn't working. One day, I pored over all the "dots" in a Starbucks, trying to connect them to come up with a potential solution. (The dots are all of the facts and factors that you're dealing with right now.) For us, the dots were factors like the way we were charging our license fees, the value we were delivering, market trends, and client feedback. After I reviewed all the data, the right answer clicked, and all the pieces came together. I had a light bulb moment about exactly how we should restructure our economic model. I called my partner and said, "Don, we're about to turn our business model on its ear."

We made the very difficult changes, which included changing our licensing fees to a fixed monthly fee, creating an open-sourced, abundance-based approach to delivering our content and raising our standards. This enabled us to generate revenue from nonproducing EOS Implementers that were using our intellectual property and maximize the personal income of each of the high-producing EOS Implementers, because their fee was capped. Our business took off and grew 40 percent every year for ten straight years after the change. Only by talking to and listening to our clients did I gain the insight to change our economic model and save our company.

Discipline #5: Always Have a Plan B

This discipline may seem redundant after the last one, but it's not. The point here is that you must have a mind-set that is ready, willing, and able to make course corrections. Know that your first plan won't be your final plan.

Discipline #4 advises that you always listen to your customer, which might very likely lead to a change in your business plan.

Discipline #5 counsels that you take your leap *knowing* changes will have to be made, so you're ready and not surprised. I always have a plan B, C, and D on the drawing board. You should too.

There's no way to predict what the change is going to be and when or why it will happen, but you do need to prepare yourself for the fact that it's going to happen. As Clayton M. Christensen says in his book *How Will You Measure Your Life?*, "You have to balance having a vision with reacting to luck, opportunities and challenges."

In his book *The Origin and Evolution of New Businesses*, Professor Amar V. Bhidé states, "Ninety-three percent of all companies that ultimately become successful have only done so after abandoning their strategy in favor of something that works."

Discipline #6: Work Hard, Really Hard

It makes me crazy when I hear "gurus" teach their easy way to build a business. Every entrepreneur I've ever talked to has told me their journey was the opposite of easy. It's counterproductive for people to believe that. This sets them up for failure. You're better off going into your leap believing it's hard and then discovering it's easier than you thought.

I've been inside hundreds of businesses and have yet to see one that takes no effort. I love it when one of my clients talks about another company, which also happens to be one of my clients, and says, "That business is so easy. I wish I had that one." I think, "Oh, if you only knew."

Frankly, if you did come up with a business that's easy to run, odds are the competition would come out of the woodwork. Within a year or two, due to such fierce competition, the business wouldn't be so easy anymore.

Here are four great quotes that have motivated me in regard to this discipline of working hard.

The first one is from Theodore Roosevelt: "It is not the critic who counts; not the man who points out how the strong man stumbles, or where the doer of deeds could have done them better. The credit belongs to the man who is actually in the arena, whose face is marred by dust and sweat and blood; who strives valiantly; who errs, who comes short again and again, because there is no effort without error and shortcoming; but who does actually strive to do the deeds; who knows great enthusiasms, the great devotions; who spends himself in a worthy cause; who at the best knows in the end the triumph of high achievement, and who at the worst, if he fails, at least fails while daring greatly, so that his place shall never be with those cold and timid souls who neither know victory nor defeat."

The second quote is from Will Smith: "The only thing that I see that is distinctly different about me is I'm not afraid to die on a treadmill . . . You might have more talent than me, you might be smarter than me, you might be sexier than me . . . But if we get on the treadmill together, there's two things: you're getting off first, or I'm going to die. It's really that simple."

This third quote is from Tommy Caldwell, the legendary rock climber and author of *The Push*: "I can suffer for and focus on the thing longer than anyone else."

The final quote is often attributed to Albert Einstein: "It's not that I'm so smart, it's just that I stay with problems longer."

Discipline #7: Take Criticism and Doubt with a Grain of Salt

Thousands of entrepreneurs who took their leap had to endure family, friends, and significant others telling them they were making a mistake. When I presented my idea for EOS Worldwide to a group of entrepreneurs who were friends and peers, all but one told me I was crazy and that it wouldn't work. Thirty-one publishers turned down my first book, *Traction*, because "there was nothing new here" and "it wouldn't sell." It has sold over half a million copies at the time of this writing.

You'll be faced with the same negative feedback. You have to take it with a grain of salt and keep pushing forward.

Someone once shared with me the story of a very successful entrepreneur who would frequently assemble a board of ten "smart people" whose opinions, he led them to believe, he valued. He met with this board on multiple occasions and presented his ideas to them. When seven out of the ten hated the idea, he knew it was a money maker. When ten out of ten hated it, he knew it was revolutionary.

Now on to Discipline #8, which is a bit different than the previous seven in that it's less tangible. It takes a little blind faith.

Discipline #8: See It Every Night

You must see your ten-year goal vividly in your mind every night before you go to bed. Most important, make sure this goal is what you want because you'll probably get it. The power of this discipline has been described thousands of ways over thousands of years. You can find it in Earl Nightingale's work *The Strangest Secret*, in which he teaches: "We become what we think about most of the time."

The classic book *Think and Grow Rich* prescribes a similar discipline for becoming successful: Simply put, where our attention goes, energy flows.

Dan Sullivan says, "Our eyes only see and our ears only hear what our brain is looking for."

In his book *You²: A High Velocity Formula for Multiplying Your Personal Effectiveness in Quantum Leaps*, Price Pritchett describes this phenomenon this way: "You must focus on ends, rather than means . . . Rivet your attention on that spot where you are to land at the end of your quantum leap . . . Once you do that, it's almost as if you magnetize yourself to the ways and means involved in the methodology for getting there. Solutions begin to appear. Answers come to you."

And if all of the above is too heady, Yogi Berra simplified this universal truth by saying, "If you don't know where you are going, you might not get there."

I've practiced this discipline for almost thirty years now with multiple businesses and many different goals with great results. I urge you to do the same. If you see something clearly in your mind, it's more likely to happen.

Here are the eight disciplines at a glance:

Discipline #1: Clarify Your Vision

Discipline #2: Decide if You're a "Partner Person"

Discipline #3: Know That the Bigger the Problem You Solve in the World, the More Successful You'll Be

Discipline #4: Get Feedback from Customers and Clients Early and Often

Discipline #5: Always Have a Plan B

Discipline #6: Work Hard, Really Hard

Discipline #7: Take Criticism and Doubt with a Grain of Salt

Discipline #8: See It Every Night

It might be helpful to keep them close by as a constant reminder on your journey.

SUMMARY

Having now read the eight disciplines, you probably see that there's no one way to take your leap and no perfect set of steps. Yet this handful of disciplines, when you're ready, will serve you well and increase your odds of success. Unfortunately, they cannot guarantee success. You may still fail. Just make sure that if you fail, you fail forward and try again.

One test reader for this manuscript, Nancy Lyons, a successful entrepreneur, urged me to address the subject of failure and resilience a bit more. She explained, "I know for me—my best lessons have come through some of the worst experiences I've had in business. I've been so close to failure that I've had to mentally prepare for losing everything. And even while running a successful business—I've had horrible years that have caused me to question everything. I know the entrepreneurs I'm closest to all have stories of failure: declaring bankruptcy and starting over, coming close to closing their doors, leveraging every last thing. Just a couple of years ago, my company had our worst year ever. I spent months back pounding the pavement myself. I called everyone I've ever met until we sold things and reset ourselves and got back on track. Now, two years later, we've had the best year ever. And in looking back, I wouldn't change a single thing. My company is better. The leadership team is tighter. We're more focused and more disciplined."

Here's a fascinating list of all of Abraham Lincoln's failures and setbacks on his journey to becoming the president of the United States in 1861:

- lost job, 1832
- defeated for Illinois General Assembly seat, 1832
- failed in business, 1833
- sweetheart Ann Rutledge died, 1835
- had nervous breakdown, 1836
- lost bid for speaker, 1838
- defeated for nomination for Congress, 1843
- rejected for commissioner of the land office, 1849
- defeated for Senate, 1854
- defeated for nomination for vice president, 1856
- defeated again for Senate, 1858

Now we'll move on to see what building your business looks like. Before we do, please take some time and answer all eight questions from Discipline #1: Capture Your Vision.

WORKSHEET

1. What am I passionate about? (Why am I doing this?)

   _____

   _____

2. What want/need am I filling for my customer/ client?

   _____

   _____

3. Who is my ideal customer? (Describe your ideal customer.)

   _____

   _____

4. What's the pricing structure for my product or service?

   _____

   _____

5. What's the number one most important goal to accomplish in ten years?

_____

_____

6. What will the business look like in three years? (Include your top-line revenue, your personal income, your profit, and ten bullet points describing exactly what your business will look like in three years.)

_____

_____

_____

_____

_____

_____

_____

_____

_____

_____

_____

_____

_____

_____

_____

_____

_____

_____

_____

_____

_____

7. What do I have to accomplish in the first year? (Include your top-line revenue, your personal income, your profit, and your three to seven most important goals.)

_____

_____

_____

_____

_____

_____

_____

_____

_____

_____

_____

_____

_____

_____

_____

8. What are the three to seven most important things I
   need to get done in the next ninety days?

_____

_____

_____

_____

_____

_____

_____

_____

_____

_____

_____

_____

_____

_____

Additional Thoughts

_____

_____

_____

_____

_____

_____

_____

_____

_____

What action can you take in the next seven days to help
you take your entrepreneurial leap?

_____

_____

_____

_____

_____

_____

_____

You can download MyVision Clarifier and all
worksheets and tools at e-leap.com.

CHAPTER 15

BUILDING YOUR BUSINESS: THE NINE STAGES

This chapter assumes you've taken your leap. You have a product or service you're selling. I'd first like to congratulate you, because you're officially an entrepreneur. Now it's time to build your business.

Once again, no book can tell you the exact steps and path you'll take to achieve your ten-year goal, because every path is different. As you might imagine, building a $100 million national restaurant chain is a lot different than building a $1 million cabinet-making company. However, every entrepreneur faces some very consistent milestones, hurdles, events, and steps along the way, and this chapter will address each of them.

Here's one entrepreneur's story of building a successful company.

Jay Wilkinson, the founder of Firespring, started his first business while still in high school. In the beginning, he charged for raking leaves, mowing lawns, and shoveling snow but eventually found his niche by providing industrial clean-up and painting services for a real estate company when people moved out of their homes and left a mess behind.

His father tells the story of looking for Jay when he was sixteen years old by trying to find him on a job site. Jay was nowhere around, but one of the young ladies painting the door of a duplex said, "I think he's at the lake." Furious with his son for shirking responsibility, he searched for him at the local lake, where Jay was found water skiing with his buddies.

"Dad," Jay said, "I made a few hundred dollars today. I charge by the job and pay people by the hour. I'm not shirking anything." Like many entrepreneurs, Jay discovered capitalism at a young age.

While in college, Jay started several more companies, most of which failed miserably. He quickly learned that ideas are useless without action and that a business is not a business until it can scale revenue. During his junior year, Jay partnered with two other entrepreneurs to start a magazine oriented to college students. This was a few years before the internet took over the world, and the premise was that every student needed to know the best places to eat, see a movie, get a haircut, go on a date, etc. This publication would be so valuable that students would hold on to it all year. Advertisers loved it, and cash flow came easy.

After two successful years, Jay and his partners moved to New York City to scale the business. Before long Jay realized that, while he had no shortage of ideas and vision, he lacked the natural wiring to manage the day-to-day details or to hold other people accountable. The partners sat down and clarified their roles, and Jay stepped completely out of finance and operations. The publication grew rapidly—to more than 1.2 million issues distributed to more than three hundred college campuses all over America. Four years later, they sold the publication and, having become a father for the first time, Jay moved back to his home state of Nebraska so his son could grow up on grass instead of concrete.

Back home in Nebraska, Jay applied all that he'd learned from his previous eight companies and launched a printing business that hit $1 million in annualized revenue in its ninth month of operation. A few years later, the internet began to change everything, and in 2001, Jay founded a software-as-a-service business to provide printing companies with templated websites that made it possible for them to do business online. A few angel investors and a large venture capital firm partnered together to invest $2.6 million in the fledgling start-up.

Jay invited three of the investors to join his board so he could soak up their wisdom. The influx of cash was used to hire a few dozen people and add sales offices in cities across the United States. Revenue exploded as the business capitalized on their first-to-market position, and they were soon closing one out of every three demos.

Then 9/11 happened.

The close rate sank to one in ten as the prospects affected by a failing economy stopped spending money. The board wanted Jay to lay off half of his team. He resisted, claiming that he would find a way to claw back the revenue. But a few months later, on a three-to-two vote, the board fired him as the CEO of his own company and reassigned him to a management committee comprised of Jay, two members of his leadership team, and two board members. It was a crushing lesson that Jay wouldn't fully appreciate for years to come.

Jay's lesson: The majority owner of any business should never give control of their board to investors. And when faced with a substantial reduction in revenue (i.e., losing a big client, a competitor lowering their prices, or changes in the market) that results in massive cash burn, you can't respond quickly enough. Cut costs immediately and don't scale back up until revenue supports it.

In the days and weeks that followed his firing, Jay—fueled by passion, grit, and humility—held the investors at bay. Behind the scenes, he started working on a plan to buy out the VC firm and brought together his team to share every detail with them so they knew exactly what was going on. Together, they created a plan that resulted in everyone in the company taking a massive pay cut. Some deferred their entire salaries because their spouses were bringing home enough money to pay the bills. Others offered young, single coworkers a spare bedroom in their homes so they could reduce rent expenses. It became clear that they were all in this together. After six months, Jay found new investors to buy out the VCs, and when he sent them the final check, he added $0.01 so he could satisfy his own expectation that "no investor should ever lose money by betting on me."

As soon as the VC firm was out, Jay stocked his board of directors with company insiders and went on about building the company. He went through an exercise to discover the company's core values, established a new purpose, set short-term and long-term goals, and began zealously communicating with the team so that each of them were made aware of every win, every loss, and every issue. By building a foundation of trust and accountability, he grew the company quickly, and in the second calendar year after the buyout, the company showed a net operating profit of more than $1 million.

When the business began hitting another ceiling a few years later, Jay implemented an operating system that resulted in his company, Firespring, tripling its revenue in three years. And the company evolved by implementing its Power of 3 Program, where it gives 1 percent of its top-line revenue to charity, 2 percent of its products and services to nonprofits, and 3 percent of its people back to the community by requiring every team member to volunteer to a cause of their choice, with pay, for one full day every month.

Today, Firespring has hundreds of employees and thousands of clients in all fifty states and fourteen countries. In 2016, *Inc.*

magazine featured Firespring as one the 50 Best Workplaces in America.

As you can see, there are many stages to building a business. We'll now address the most common to help you stay one step ahead of the barriers that slow or prevent many entrepreneurs from growing their businesses to their full potentials.

STAGE 1: GENERATING CASH

You don't have a business without cash flow. To generate cash, you must sell something. Until you've done that, you've not proven your product or service has value.

Don't fall into the trap of your mom, dad, or anyone else telling you that you have a great idea. Until customers or clients start paying you, you have nothing.

The day you launch your business, the number one goal you must obsess about is generating cash. Even with forty other things competing for your attention—marketing, a product failure, paying bills, hiring someone, your vision, your customers, your phone ringing, your website, signing a contract, needing a new laptop—what matters most is generating cash.

Welcome to entrepreneurship.

STAGE 2: HIRING AN INTEGRATOR

Almost twenty years ago, I made the discovery that most true entrepreneurs must be counterbalanced with an "Integrator." If you have all six essential entrepreneurial traits, then it's almost certain you need an integrator. Unfortunately, entrepreneurs are rarely great at the day-to-day running of a business and managing the people. Their genetic encoding is big picture, big ideas, creating, growing. On the other hand, integrators are great at the day-to-day running of a business, managing and holding people accountable, and harmoniously integrating resources. They execute your vision.

I make this an early (stage 2) issue in building your business because some entrepreneurs are proactive enough to launch their business with their Integrator already in place. This can be an employee or an equity partner, depending on whether you prefer a partner or not.

When I launched EOS Worldwide, I knew I couldn't do it without an Integrator. So the very first thing I did was find one. You don't need an integrator to start your business. Most entrepreneurs don't, but at some point, you'll most likely need this counterpart, whether on day one or in year ten. Many entrepreneurs play both roles for years until they absolutely need to hire an integrator, while some join forces right out of the shoot.

When you feel ready to find your integrator counterpart, I urge you to read the book I wrote, *Rocket Fuel*, with coauthor

Mark C. Winters. It will show you exactly how to do it. And help you to be a better entrepreneur.

Joel Pearlman and Rob Dube of imageOne started their business as an entrepreneur-integrator dynamic duo and fifty-fifty partners. By contrast, Todd Sachse of Sachse Construction built his company to over $100 million over twenty years before he decided to hire an integrator.

Reading *Rocket Fuel* will help you decide the right time for you to bring on an integrator, and exactly how to do so.

STAGE 3: DISCOVERING YOUR CORE VALUES

You must discover your core values before you hire your first employee. Core values are the three to seven timeless guiding principles on which you'll build your company. Core values are what define your company's culture. A strong culture helps a company endure and be great. In the words of business guru Peter Drucker, "Culture eats strategy for breakfast."

The reason you must know your company's core values is that when you hire your first—or your hundredth—employee, you must hire only people who possess your company's core values. This is the only way to protect and maintain a strong company culture.

Here's the good news: your company's core values already exist. They're discovered rather than created. The process is a matter of uncovering what your three to seven core values are. To help you along, here's a list of some real-world core values:

- unequivocal excellence
- continually strives for perfection
- wins
- does the right thing
- compassion
- honesty and integrity
- hungry for achievement
- is enthusiastic, energetic, tenacious, and competitive
- encourages individual ability and creativity
- maintains accountability
- services the customer above all else
- works hard
- is never satisfied
- is interested in continuous self-improvement
- helps first
- exhibits professionalism
- encourages individual initiative
- growth-oriented
- treats everyone with respect
- provides opportunity based on merit: no one is entitled to anything
- has creativity, dreams, and imagination
- has personal integrity

- isn't cynical
- exhibits modesty and humility alongside confidence
- practices fanatical attention to consistency and detail
- is committed
- understands the value of reputation
- is fun
- is fair
- encourages teamwork

Choose the three to seven that most resonate with you. These are your nonnegotiable guiding principles. Add anything you feel is missing from the list and then wordsmith them so they best suit you and your company.

Let's say you conclude that your core values are these four things:

1. Do the right thing
2. Have fun
3. Work hard
4. Be growth-oriented

With these four core values clearly defined, you must make them the rite of passage into your company. Hire only people who possess these core values. If you hire someone by mistake who you later discover doesn't share these four core values, you must remove them quickly. Otherwise, they will corrode your culture.

This is an early-stage discipline, because in the building of a company, the most common mistake new entrepreneurs make is hiring or partnering with the wrong people. They soon find themselves involved in a nightmare of trying to get out of a bad partnership or removing employees who don't fit. I share this because my clients, in the first year of the process with me, have to get rid of an average of 20 percent of their employees due to hiring mistakes from the past.

Don't make the mistake of hiring your brother, cousin, friend, or anyone who doesn't have your core values merely because you need a body right now or you feel you can trust them. Don't hire anyone unless you're certain that their core values match yours.

STAGE 4: HOLDING YOURSELF ACCOUNTABLE

As soon as possible, identify the three most important numbers you must hit every week to achieve your annual goals. Every business has them. These are the three numbers that, if hit on a weekly basis, will enable you to achieve your one-year plan.

In your first year, these three numbers will almost always be sales- and marketing-related, because that's the lifeblood of all businesses. Examples of marketing and sales numbers include the following:

- number of visitors to your website
- number of followers
- number of clicks
- number of phone calls
- number of appointments or meetings
- number of referrals
- number of sales closed
- revenue generated for the week

Decide which three numbers are most important. Which ones, if you hit them every week, will ensure your company's success? Then track those numbers weekly and make sure they're hit. If you hit them, celebrate. If you don't, figure out how to make it up by next week. As mathematician Karl Pearson said, "That which is measured improves. That which is measured and reported, improves exponentially." Simply put, if you aren't hitting your numbers every week, you aren't going to achieve your vision.

STAGE 5: COMMUNICATING FREQUENTLY WITH YOUR EMPLOYEES

Once you have employees, it's vital you stay connected. One of the most common mistakes entrepreneurs make is assuming that everyone knows what's going on. As a result, the entrepreneur starts taking employee communication for granted.

In almost every case when I start working with a client, the biggest issue they're facing is their employees feel disconnected. You must start the habit of frequent communication as soon as possible. The right hand always needs to know what the left hand is doing. You can't achieve your vision without great people all rowing in the same direction.

This is actually a simple discipline and involves doing only five routines:

1. Meet every week to make sure all numbers and priorities are on track and to solve that week's relevant issues.
2. Meet every quarter to review the vision, set quarterly priorities, and solve longer-term issues.
3. Communicate one-on-one as necessary.
4. Give constant feedback—both good and bad—to your employees.
5. Say thank you often. Let your employees know you appreciate them.

STAGE 6: HAVING A
PLAN B, C, AND D

Remember: your first plan won't be your final plan. I hope you're convinced of this by now. You'll probably need to make changes to plan A. Again, while building your business, constantly listen to your clients, get feedback, and make sure you're providing value. Your number one job is to create raving fans. By being obsessive about this goal, you'll quickly learn when some facet of your product, service, or business model isn't working, and therefore you can make the necessary changes immediately.

If you're a visionary, problem solver, and risk taker—three of the six essential entrepreneurial traits—you'll have a sixth sense for seeing where trends are heading and have the foresight to evolve, change, morph, or pivot when the business model isn't working. Also, if outside forces—such as government regulation, fierce competition, and industry or economic changes—throw you a curveball, the discipline of keeping your ear to the ground and having a pulse on your customers will help you make the correct changes to plan A. Never stop paying attention and obsessing until the day you retire or sell your company.

STAGE 7: STAYING IN YOUR PERSONAL SWEET SPOT

As you launch and build your business, you'll need to wear many hats. This is normal. Marketing, selling, providing the service, paying the bills, and so on. Where most entrepreneurs get stuck is they continue to do it all, exceed their capacity, and implode. As your business grows, you'll reach an inflection point where you can't do everything anymore. Once you reach capacity, you can't market and sell as much, because you're busy with other tasks. Growth stops, and you hit the ceiling. Most entrepreneurs become stalled and stagnate for years in misery.

To avoid this common barrier to growth, when you reach capacity, you must learn to hire a person to take over a responsibility you're handling and then delegate it. You have four fundamental responsibilities when you start your business—marketing, sales, operations, and finance. Once you reach capacity and it's time to hire someone to free you up, always make sure you hire someone for the responsibility you enjoy the least—let's say finance. The following org chart gives you a simple model to understand what I'm talking about.

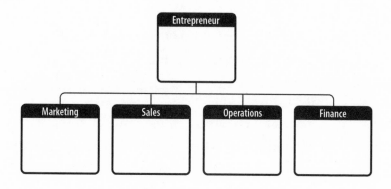

If you like finance the least, then your first hire should be for the finance role. Let's say you do that, and the company continues to grow. Once you reach capacity again, it's time to hire someone to handle the responsibility you like second least, let's say operations. You now hire an operations person. When you reach capacity again, hire the next employee and so on, until someday you have four employees—or maybe a thousand.

The process is quite simple. Your job is to make sure you hire just before you reach capacity so that you don't stop growth. Again, make sure you hire for what you like the least, and someday you'll find yourself doing only the things you love and using your talents to their fullest.

If at any point you're at capacity and can't afford to hire someone, then there's something wrong with your economic model. Either you aren't charging enough, you're being commoditized, you're overpaying yourself, or your spending is out of control. With all that said, I've never met an entrepreneur who hasn't struggled to make payroll a few times.

STAGE 8: PREVENTING YOUR BUSINESS FROM GETTING AWAY FROM YOU

My biggest fear in writing this book is making things too simple for you, removing so many obstacles that you grow bigger than you should. Clients have said to me more times than I can remember that they wish they'd met me and learned this stuff twenty years earlier. These are very successful entrepreneurs in their forties, fifties, and sixties who are just learning what I'm telling you right now. They know how much further along they'd be if they'd learned it in their twenties or thirties.

While I could not be more excited about sharing this book with you, I do wonder if you'll know when enough is enough. As David Packard of Hewlett-Packard put it, "A successful company is more likely to die of indigestion from too much opportunity than starvation from too little."

Let's pretend your ten-year goal is to build a $10 million, highly profitable, high-end local home-entertainment installation business with twenty employees, which allows you time for your family.

After five years, you become well-known, have raving fans, are winning business awards, receiving press, and collecting accolades. You get so caught up in the hype that someone talks you into opening other locations in other states. In addition, your clients love your service so much, and you're already working in their homes installing home-entertainment systems, so it just makes sense to install alarm systems and computer equipment as well. Then you find yourself in ten years with a $50 million company installing alarms, computers, and high-end home-entertainment systems in five states. You have no passion for computers or alarm systems. You're traveling constantly and must be responsible for a hundred employees. You're not very profitable, and you're miserable.

You might be surprised by the number of times this scenario happens to entrepreneurs.

That's why it's important to decide now what you really want in the future, so the future doesn't get away from you. So many entrepreneurs have a run of success, start adding products or services they never should have, or have more employees than they ever wanted. They get away from what they love to do, what they're passionate about, and what their company's true sweet spot is.

Many people have a hard time saying no to opportunities. Just remember what Warren Buffett said: "The difference between successful people and *really* successful people is that really successful people say no to almost everything."

One of my major jobs in helping clients is to refocus them back on their core business by getting rid of unnecessary business units and products or services, as well as bad clients.

STAGE 9: CAPITALIZING ON COACHING, TRAINING, AND MENTORING

The value of a trusted advisor cannot be underestimated. The highest performers in the world have a coach or mentor. We've already covered the benefits of finding a mentor, and in addition, I would highly recommend several other steps in learning. First, the day you start earning the qualifying annual $200,000 personal income, join the Strategic Coach® Program. Dan Sullivan created this program, which has helped thousands of entrepreneurs become incredibly successful. I've participated in the program for over twenty years. It has changed my life, and I'm confident it will have the same huge impact on yours. You can learn more about it at strategiccoach.com.

Once you have employees, I urge you to read my first book, *Traction: Get a Grip on Your Business*, which will teach you how to implement the "operating system" I created—EOS, the Entrepreneurial Operating System—into your business. Almost a hundred thousand companies all over the world use the EOS tools.

EOS will help you run a better business; it will show you how to structure your organization, prioritize and manage data and people better, and solve issues and execute your vision faster. You can learn more about EOS at eosworldwide.com. Most of my clients say, "I wish I had EOS when I started my business."

Once you reach a million dollars in revenue, I urge you to

look into peer-group organizations, where you can meet with five to fifteen other like-minded entrepreneurs monthly to share with, learn from, and help one another. These organizations have also had a huge impact on tens of thousands of entrepreneurs' lives, as well as mine.

Some examples of peer-group organizations are Entrepreneurs' Organization (EO), Young Presidents' Organization (YPO), Women Presidents' Organization (WPO), Vistage, The Alternative Board (TAB), National Association of Women Business Owners (NAWBO), and the Young Entrepreneur Council (YEC).

So there you have it. The nine stages. The exciting journey that is building your business. While you know by now that this is hard, it's the most enjoyable, rewarding, wild, exhilarating, challenging, and scary ride you'll ever take. I wouldn't trade it for anything.

TOP TWENTY LESSONS FROM SUCCESSFUL ENTREPRENEURS

As part of my research for this book, I interviewed many entrepreneurs and asked them to give you their advice. I've broken this advice into two groups of ten lessons.

The first ten lessons are answers to the question, "What advice would you give an entrepreneur-in-the-making considering taking a leap?"

The second ten lessons are answers to the question, "Looking back, what advice would you give yourself before you took your leap (knowing what you know now)?"

Here were the most common answers.

What Advice Would You Give an Entrepreneur-in-the-Making Considering Taking a Leap?

1. Do what you love.
2. Your value to your customer has to be very clear.
3. Don't be afraid: do it early. I wish I had started earlier!
4. Ask for help.
5. Just do it! Being a crappy entrepreneur is better than having a real job! And don't think that your first business is always going to be your last business.
6. Do as many favors as you can. Build as many relationships as possible.
7. Follow your instincts.
8. Surround yourself with truth tellers.
9. Persevere, be willing to go all in 100 percent, work your ass off, and meet whatever challenges arise and learn from them.
10. Know what you're good at and stay in your lane.

Looking Back, What Advice Would You Give Yourself Before You Took Your Leap (Knowing What You Know Now)?

1. Pick your partners carefully: it's a marriage. Think ten to twenty years out.
2. Start sooner.
3. Be vulnerable, be real, and put yourself out there sooner.
4. Take financial security/money off the table sooner.
5. Ignore societal norms; behave like you know it's going to work out.
6. Hire the best people sooner.
7. Be more focused on relationships.
8. Have amazing, smart, talented people around you.
9. You have your own gift. You aren't supposed to be good at everything.
10. Stay focused. Don't get distracted by shiny stuff.

SUMMARY

At this point, we've achieved the objective of this book. We have gone from confirming that you're an entrepreneur-in-the-making, to showing you a glimpse of what your life could look like if you take the leap, to then showing you the path to becoming a successful entrepreneur. Mission accomplished!

However, I believe that it's important to add one last chapter to help you stay motivated and educated. As an entrepreneur, you need to break through barriers constantly and keep growing for a lifetime.

Before we go to the final chapter, please take a few minutes to capture your thoughts, ideas, and concerns from this chapter.

WORKSHEET

What actions can you take in the next seven days to help you build your business?

CHAPTER 16

A LIFETIME OF GROWTH, LEARNING, AND MOTIVATION

You're the culmination of the books you read and the people you hang around with. This chapter introduces you to some great resources for your journey. An important caution is that, given all you'll read, hear, watch, and learn in educating yourself as an entrepreneur, please understand that if you try to do everything you learn about, it will twist you in a knot and potentially put you out of business.

Not all advice is for everyone. You can find a lot of information out there, and one size does not fit all. As Dr. James Dobson states, "The same boiling water that hardens the egg will soften the carrot." You have to be selective and trust your gut. Glean what's best for your vision, your plan, and your company.

With that in mind, here are ten ideas to keep you ahead of the game and charging forward:

1. **Read one nonfiction book a month. Here's a list to get started:**

- *Traction*, Gino Wickman
- *Rocket Fuel*, Gino Wickman and Mark C. Winters
- *Think and Grow Rich*, Napoleon Hill
- *The Millionaire Next Door*, Thomas J. Stanley and William D. Danko
- *Good to Great*, Jim Collins
- *The 7 Habits of Highly Effective People*, Steven R. Covey
- *Unique Ability*, Catherine Nomura, Dan Sullivan, Julia Waller and Shannon Waller
- *The Young Entrepreneur's Guide to Starting and Running a Business*, Steve Mariotti
- *The Lean Startup*, Eric Ries
- *How to Win Friends and Influence People*, Dale Carnegie
- *Great by Choice*, Jim Collins and Jerry I. Porras
- *Built to Last*, Jim Collins and Jerry Poras
- *The Five Dysfunctions of a Team*, Patrick Lencioni
- *The E-Myth Revisited*, Michael Gerber
- *Small Giants*, Bo Burlingham
- *The Startup Owners Manual*, Steve Blank
- *Crushing It*, Gary Vaynerchuk
- *Emotional Intelligence 2.0*, Travis Bradberry and Jean Greaves
- *Essentialism*, Greg McKeown

- *Zero to One*, Peter Thiel
- *Principles*, Ray Dalio
- *Start with Why*, Simon Sinek
- *The Hard Thing About Hard Things*, Ben Horowitz
- *Rich Dad, Poor Dad*, Robert Kiyosaki

2. **Read biographies of successful entrepreneurs**:

- *Screw It, Let's Do It*, Richard Branson
- *Steve Jobs*, Walter Isaacson
- *Shoe Dog*, Phil Knight
- *Pour Your Heart Into It*, Howard Schultz, Starbucks
- Thomas Edison (multiple books)
- Walt Disney (multiple books)
- *I Invented the Modern Age: The Rise of Henry Ford*, Richard Snow
- *Made in America*, Sam Walton
- George Washington (multiple books)

3. **Listen to your favorite podcasts**:

- How I Built This with Guy Raz
- The Tim Ferriss Show
- The Multiplier Mindset with Dan Sullivan
- I Love Marketing with Joe Polish and Dean Jackson
- The School of Greatness with Lewis Howes

- Growth Now Movement
- The Gary Vee Audio Experience with Gary Vaynerchuk
- Entrepreneurs on Fire
- Cool Things Entrepreneurs Do
- The Nice Guys on Business
- MFCEO Project
- No Quit Living
- Youpreneur
- Akimbo with Seth Godin
- The Liberator
- Avanti Entrepreneur with David Mammano

4. **Watch online videos on leadership, motivation, entrepreneurship, TED Talks, and running a business. Just search those words and you'll find thousands of videos to watch.**

5. **Read business blogs:**

- EOS Worldwide, eosworldwide.com/blog
- Score, score.org/blog
- Derek Sivers, sivers.org/blog
- Entrepreneur on Fire, eofire.com/blog
- Foundr, foundr.com/blog
- Tim Ferriss, tim.blog
- Close, blog.close.com

- HubSpot Sales, blog.hubspot.com/sales
- Sales Hacker, saleshacker.com/library
- Abundance 360, diamandis.com/blog
- Seth Godin, seths.blog
- Lean Startup Co., leanstartup.co

6. **Surround yourself with entrepreneurs. Coffee meetings, networking, find a mentor, join a peer group, get into The Strategic Coach® Program.**

7. **Know thyself. Learn your MO (who you are, how you operate, etc.). There are great tools to help you do this:**

- Kolbe A™ Index
- DiSC
- Myers-Briggs
- Culture Index
- Strengths Finder
- Learn about Emotional Intelligence
- Go to a therapist

8. **Take some "coffee shop" time. I recommend every entrepreneur take one to two hours a week in a coffee shop for thinking time to work "on" your business and to review your business vision, plan, and goals.**

9. Read inspirational quotes. Here are some favorites:

- "Our deepest fear is not that we are inadequate. Our deepest fear is that we are powerful beyond measure. It is our light, not our darkness, that most frightens us . . . Your playing small does not serve the world. There's nothing enlightened about shrinking so that other people won't feel insecure around you. We are all meant to shine as children do . . . It's not just in some of us; it is in everyone. And as we let our own lights shine, we unconsciously give others permission to do the same. As we are liberated from our own fear, our presence automatically liberates others."—Marianne Williamson

- "The best revenge is massive success."—Frank Sinatra

- "An entrepreneur is someone who jumps off a cliff and builds a plane on the way down."—Reid Hoffman

- "You must be very patient, very persistent. The world isn't going to shower gold coins on you just because you have a good idea. You are going to have to work like crazy to bring that idea to the attention of the people. They are not going to buy it unless they know about it."—Herb Kelleher

- "The very first company I started failed with a great bang. The second one failed a little bit less, but still failed. The third one, you know, proper failed, but it was kind of ok. I recovered quickly. Number four almost didn't fail. I still didn't really feel great, but it did ok. Number five was PayPal."—Max Levchin

- "When you're surrounded by people who share a passionate commitment around a common purpose, anything is possible."—Howard E. Schultz
- "I had all of the disadvantages required for success." —Larry Ellison
- "The way to get started is to quit talking and begin doing."—Walt Disney
- "If you really want to do something, you'll find a way. If you don't, you'll find an excuse."—Jim Rohn
- "Fall seven times and stand up eight."—Japanese proverb
- "If you're going through hell, keep going."—Source unknown
- "A real entrepreneur is somebody who has no safety net underneath them."—Henry Kravis

10. Look at the balance in your bank account. That should motivate you to get to work.

For an updated list of books, podcasts, blogs, and other resources, go to e-leap.com.

So there it is, my thirty years of experience in 200 pages. I had a blast writing it, and I hope it helps you become an incredibly successful entrepreneur. I'll now put the point of this book in a nutshell.

Becoming an entrepreneur is not something you do—it's something you are. It's not about writing a business plan, raising money, getting business cards, following a methodical plan, and making a living. It's about possessing the six essential traits. And if you do, your journey is typically four major steps:

Step 1—Having an idea, solution, product, service, light bulb moment that ignites you

Step 2—Taking the entrepreneurial leap to sell your idea to the world

Step 3—Fighting like hell for ten years

Step 4—Emerging a successful, battle-tested entrepreneur (hopefully . . . remember the odds)

Again, there's no perfect, detailed, step-by-step process for becoming a successful entrepreneur. What this book provides is the ability to confirm that you have the essential traits. And if so, offers you clarity about your future and all of your available options; and then insight into college, finding your passion and mentorship—along with disciplines to help you take a better leap and increase your odds of success through those four major steps.

To help you write and think about the concepts in this book along your journey, I created the Leap Journal, which is a summary of the teachings in each chapter, along with journal pages to capture your most important thinking. You can find it at e-leap.com.

In summary, I have three wishes for you, or better said, impassioned pleas.

The first is that you save at least 15 percent of everything you personally earn. Far too many entrepreneurs spend everything they make, counting on a big payday when they sell their businesses, which unfortunately never happens for them, and they end up with nothing. If you save at least 15 percent of everything you earn from this day forward, odds are you'll have a large nest egg for retirement.

And then maybe the icing on the cake will be a big payday when you sell your business. But don't bet everything on that. Sadly, most entrepreneurs die broke because they fall into the trap of thinking their business will be the goose that lays the golden egg forever. They spend everything they make buying houses, boats, and cars.

Unfortunately, I suffered from this in my early thirties. I hope you learn from my mistake. My goal was always to be to a millionaire by the time I was thirty. At thirty-one, I achieved my goal and was worth $1.2M (missed it by a year), and by thirty-three, I was flat broke and $200,000 in debt. This was when I was creating EOS. It was during the dot-com crash of 2000. I had very risky investments that went south, bills to pay, and no income. I was trying to build a new business. I had no safety net, a five- and eight-year-old, and thank God, a very supportive wife. That loss could have all been avoided if I had been more fiscally responsible. Fortunately, that was a turning point for me, and I've been financially disciplined ever since. I repeat: please save at least 15 percent of everything you earn, and invest it wisely!

On the positive side, if you're fiscally responsible, the data speaks for itself. In a 2014 analysis of data on over 60 million households by CEG Worldwide and Wealth Engine, published in "The State of the Affluent 2014," 75 percent of households with investable assets of $5–$25 million are business owners, and 90 percent of households with over $25 million of investable assets are business owners.

My second wish, and passionate plea, is that you live your ideal life. This is the goal for every one of our clients at EOS Worldwide. It's defined by the following:

1. Doing what you love
2. Working with people you love
3. Making an impact
4. Being compensated appropriately
5. Having time for your other passions

If you apply what I've laid out in this book, you can make those five aspects of an ideal life come true. I see entrepreneurs achieving them every day.

And third, please make a commitment to yourself and fill in the following blank right now with your ten-year goal.

In ten years, I will _____

_____

_____

_____

_____

I wish you tremendous success on your path, and I look forward to writing about your story someday.

Stay focused.

Acknowledgments

This book would not have been possible without the help and guidance of the following people. I cannot thank them enough for the impact they have had on my life. My heartfelt appreciation goes out to them.

Kathy, my strong and beautiful wife. I could not do what I do without your belief and support. I appreciate and love you with all of my heart.

Alexis, my incredibly wise daughter. You are as beautiful on the inside as you are on the outside. Your conscientiousness makes me so proud and you make me smile every day.

Gino, my quick-witted son. You are an engineer with an incredible personality. Thank you for always making me laugh so hard. I am so very proud of you.

Linda Wickman, my mom, for teaching me to be independent, for your amazing quiet strength, wisdom, and inspiration.

You always make me feel so loved. I think about you every day and love you very much.

Floyd Wickman, my dad and my life mentor. This book would not exist without you. You are the entrepreneur's entrepreneur. You have taught me most of what I know about communicating with people, be it one or one thousand. You exemplify every principle in this book.

Neil Pardun, my father-in-law, for teaching me that it is possible to possess wealth and remain humble. You've helped me keep my feet on the ground all these years. You are a rare and special person. I am forever changed through your example.

Ed Escobar, my first business partner, for pushing hard and finally convincing my dad to let me into his company. Thanks for being so tough on me in my twenties. I now see how that transformed me. I am on this path because of your belief in me.

Mike Pallin, whom I truly believe is my guardian angel. You always place in front of me exactly what I need at that point in my life. You single handedly altered the course of my life three separate times.

Karen Grooms, the world's greatest business manager. Thanks for holding all of the pieces together and protecting me from distractions for twenty-five years.

Curt Rager and Bob Shenefelt, for being amazing sounding boards and for constantly challenging me. Our annual trip to the mountains gives me tremendous clarity. You are lifers.

Don Tinney, the best business partner a guy could have.

Thanks for fighting the good fight with me for fifteen years. We built something great together.

Sam Cupp, my business mentor, for teaching me most of what I know about business. I could not have pulled off that turnaround without your guidance. I hope I have done you proud with this book. I miss you greatly since your untimely passing.

Michael Gerber, it was your work that inspired me the earliest and the most. You are the original entrepreneur thought leader.

Dan Sullivan, for helping me discover my Unique Ability® and showing me how to build a life around it. You have made a great impact on my life. You are truly the coach of all coaches.

Verne Harnish, for being a pioneer and showing me that there is a place out there for my craft. Thank you for your passion and the impact you have had on the entrepreneurial world.

Mr. Sarkisian, Mr. Long, and the late Larry LaFever, for looking at me and treating me as the person I would become when I was a teenager. You gave me confidence, and for that I am forever grateful.

Mike Paton and Kelly Knight, for succeeding Don and I in EOS Worldwide, and allowing us to pursue our next passions.

My support team, Lisa Pisano and Kristen Froehlich, for keeping everything running like a Swiss watch.

All of the people in my EOS world, the EOS Worldwide leadership team, and all of my EOS clients. Thanks for twenty amazing years.

Interviewees, contributors, and test readers, thank you for your insight. You are forever a part of this book: Zach Albertson, David Allen, Scott Bade, Steve Barone, Thom Barry, Mackinley Bassett, Chris Bean, Anthony Benton, Joseph Benton, Ron Blank, Ted Bradshaw, Amy Bruske, Alex Burkulas, Ian Burnstein, Steven Carse, Darton Case, Jacob Cini, Ashley Clegg, Kaitlyn Cole, Nahshon Cook-Nelson, Paul Corpus, Teá Cushman, Mark D'Andreta, Ellyn Davidson, Logan Dube, Rob Dube, Craig Erlich, Jonah Erlich, Eric Ersher, Doug Etkin, Jay Feldman, Darren Findling, Ryan Findling, Kristen Froehlich, Nancy Geenen, Gary Goerke, Karen Grooms, Doug Hamburger, Joe Haney, Dan Haynes, Gretchen Hopp Doyle, Dan Israel, Kelly Knight, Kevin Kononenko, Jeff Laethem, Drew Levine, Aleana Loyd, Francy Lucido, Jared Lujan, Nancy Lyons, Joe Mackey, Anthony Marini, Kris Marshall, Keith Meadows, Michael Nehra, Ethan Neuhoff, Mike Oppedahl, Necole Parker-Green, Joel Pearlman, Lisa Pisano, Eddie Pobur Jr., Curtis Rager, Gary Ran, Matt Rossetti, Chad Rubner, Shayla Rucker, Joe Saad, Todd Sachse, Marc Schechter, Charlie Sheridan, Nicholas Sheridan, Sam Simon, Richard Simtob, Jada Skalak, Marisa Smith, Jesmarie Soto, Shawn Stafford, Dominick Stanca, Max Steir, Dan Sullivan, Shelly Sun, Rob Tamblyn, Pat Tierney, Trevor Tierney, Ninad Tipnis, Jimmy Tocco, Mike Uckele, Clay Upton, Bob Verdun, George Victor, Isabella Villanueva, Zac Voss, Zach Wardlaw, Terrell White, Jay Wilkinson, Jason Williford, Jackie Wilson, and Stu Wolff.

My publisher, Glenn Yeffeth, and the team at BenBella Books; my editor, John Paine of John Paine Editorial Services; my illustrator, Drew Robinson of Spork Design Inc.; JT McCormick and the team at Scribe Media for help with the manuscript; and my fact checker, Veronica Maddocks.

About the Author

Photo by Arising Images (www.ArisingImages.com)

GINO WICKMAN has had a passion for entrepreneurship for more than three decades. His purpose is to help entrepreneurs get everything they want from their businesses while giving them freedom, the ability to be creative, and the tools to make an impact on the world. He has built, ran, and sold two companies. He is the author of six books, which have sold more than one million copies. He created EOS (The Entrepreneurial Operating System®), which is used by almost 100,000 companies worldwide. He also leads workshops and delivers keynote addresses.